CHEFS OF DISTINCTION
worldwide

volume two

with a foreword by Anton Mosimann OBE

Published in the United Kingdom by

Ptarmigan Publishing Ltd

46 New Park Street Devizes Wiltshire SN10 1DT
UK

Telephone   +44 (0)1380 728700

Facsimile   +44 (0)1380 728701

E mail   enquiries@distinctionworld.com

Web site   www.chefsofdistinction.com

Publisher & managing director   Mark Hodson

Editing, design, and pre-press:

Mark Dawson

Colour origination and print:

Butler and Tanner, Frome

ISBN 1 90412 212 4

British Library Cataloguing in Publication Data. A catalogue record for this book is available from the British Library.

CHEFS OF DISTINCTION
worldwide

volume two

www.chefsofdistinction.com

All chefs of distinction have a passion for good food and a generosity of spirit in wanting to share their creations with like minded people. I have been very fortunate in that during my travels I have sampled cuisines from every corner of the globe and savoured the essence that makes regions unique; whether it is a noodle stand in Tokyo, an English inglenook, or in the grandest hotels of the world.

Many establishments featured here stand sentinel in their cities, but at the heart of each one of them is the kitchen. The 66 recipes pay homage to their own traditions and heritage. The excitement and passion essential to good cooking is in all of them: emotions that continue to inspire cooks everywhere to higher aspirations.

Hotel chefs have a demanding task, as I know from my own experience. Food plays a crucial role in ensuring guests have a happy and contended stay, whether they demand a gourmet experience or the most basic of 'comfort foods'. Whatever it is, only the finest ingredients will suffice.

The recipes in Chefs of Distinction Worldwide Volume 2 are favourite dishes with many guests of the featured hotels and I hope that they will become your signature dishes too.

Anton Mosimann OBE

Trio of scrambled eggs
with vegetable crisp and Parmesan fingers   12

Carpaccio of golden beetroot with herb gnocchi,
tarragon hollandaise, beetroot and cumin sabayon   14

"St Peters fish pot"
A steamed pot of freshest seafood
over a bed of virgin olive mash with a saffron jus   16

Chiffonade of vegetables and shellfish
flavoured with fresh truffle   18

Mussel soup with saffron sprigs   20

Ravioli with raw scampi, tomato filtering and Caciottina cheese   22

Egg noodle wrapped tiger prawns with exotic fruit tian   24

Crispy fried dragon prawns with mandarin orange coriander salsa,
longan filled with prawn and chilli salsa on lime jelly   26

Shrimp Chanjie with a roasted coconut dip   28

Seared crayfish and tiger prawn
with spiced coconut curry cream   30

Rosette of tiger shrimp with sesame butter   32

Seared scallops, sweet potato, pineapple,
coconut and asian spiced foam   34

Panaché of roasted scallops and foie gras, sauce Sauternes   36

Lobster escabèche with candied olives and black olive emulsion   38

Butter poached lobster with cardamom, coriander and basmati rice   40

Spring roll of lemon sole with salmon mousse,
sautéed scallops and a red pepper and tomato dressing   42

Turbot squares on a seafood and asparagus bed   44

ABBEY WELL®
ON CHIPPENDALE

pure inspiration

ABBEY WELL®

NATURAL MINERAL WATER

The love of beautiful things, both man made and natural, are rarely brought together in such complete harmony.

If you are fortunate enough to have such a beautiful piece of original furniture by Chippendale, one of our most respected and gifted furniture makers of the eighteenth century, you are indeed lucky.

To have enjoyed the pure, clean taste of ABBEY WELL®, which fell at least 3000 years ago, as rain or snow before the age of pollution, you will also have experienced the ultimate in natural refreshment.

ABBEY WELL® natural mineral water, Still or Sparkling, is available to discerning, consumers everywhere.

The Essence of Quality

Trio of scrambled eggs
with vegetable crisp and Parmesan fingers

PHILIPPE AUDONNET

HOTEL D'ANGLETERRE

Geneva, Switzerland

per serving

scrambled eggs
3 eggs
1 scampi
5g caviar
5g smoked salmon
50g butter
50ml single cream
1 pinch chives

Parmesan fingers
1 slice toast
5g grated Parmesan

vegetable crisps
beetroot
carrot
cabbage
celery
leek
aubergine

olive oil
butter

For the vegetable crisps, slice the vegetables thinly lengthwise (you will need two slices per serving). For the cabbage and leek use two leaves. Blanch each vegetable separately in boiling salted water for 30 seconds, then refresh in very cold water. Lay out the slices on a baking tray and cook in the oven at 90°C for 2 to 3 hours until they are dry and crisp. These crisps can be stored at room temperature for 3 or 4 days.

For the Parmesan fingers, cut each slice of toast into 6 fingers and top with the grated Parmesan. Heat under a salamander or grill until browned.

For the scrambled eggs, carefully take the top off each egg and empty it into a bowl. Wash the eggshells gently, but well, with clean water and place in egg cups. Pan fry the scampi in olive oil, butter and salt, then slice open along the length.

Melt 25g butter in a pan, then add the cream, salt and the 3 egg yolks and whites. Cook over a gentle heat until the eggs are soft and creamy, then stir in another 25g of butter. Half fill each shell with scrambled egg: add caviar to one egg, smoked salmon to the second, and scampi to the third. Top up with the remaining scrambled egg, then finish off again with caviar, smoked salmon and scampi. Arrange the eggs, Parmesan fingers and vegetable crisps as shown in the photograph.

Carpaccio of golden beetroot with herb gnocchi, tarragon hollandaise, beetroot and cumin sabayon

serves 6 as a starter

carpaccio
6 golden beetroots
100g rock salt

herb gnocchi
1kg Ratte potatoes
4-5 egg yolks
100g plain flour
100g chopped mixed herbs
(parsley, tarragon, chervil, dill and
coriander)
200g table salt
Freshly grated nutmeg
100g grated Gruyère

sabayon
200ml beetroot juice (red)
1 whole egg
100ml chicken stock
sugar to taste
ground cumin

hollandaise
100ml tarragon vinegar
6 peppercorns
3 juniper berries
tarragon stalks
reduced together to form 2
tablespoon of strained liquor
250g clarified butter
2 egg yolks
30g chopped blanched tarragon

Bake the golden beetroots at 180°C on the rock salt until they are soft.

For the gnocchi, bake the potatoes on the salt and when cooked pass through a fine sieve. Allow to cool slightly. Add the flour, herbs and egg yolks; mix well and season with nutmeg and black pepper, but no salt. Roll out the mixture on a lightly floured surface and then cut into triangles to form the gnocchi. Bring a pan of lightly salted water to the boil, add the gnocchi and gently simmer until they rise to the surface. Remove from the water and drain, then transfer to an oiled sheet.

For the sabayon, place all the ingredients in a metal bowl and whisk over simmering water until thick and frothy.

For the Hollandaise, whisk the egg yolks and vinegar reduction until ribbon-like, then remove from the heat. Slowly whisk in the clarified butter, add the tarragon, then season.

To plate, slice the beetroot very finely and cover the plate with one layer. Grill the gnocchi with a little of the Gruyère cheese and place over the beetroot carpaccio. Garnish with pea shoots and the tarragon hollandaise. Finish with the beetroot sabayon and a little tarragon vinaigrette over the plate.

ROBERT THOMPSON
WINTERINGHAM FIELDS
Lincolnshire, England

"St Peters fish pot"
A steamed pot of freshest seafood
over a bed of virgin olive mash with a saffron jus

Ian McDonald

SOAR MILL COVE HOTEL
Devon, England

serves 2

6 mussels,
scrubbed with beard removed

6 raw prawns,
peeled & tract removed

6 scallops, cut & cleaned
with muscle removed

1 500g John Dory, filleted

6 saffron stamen

250ml double cream

250ml dry white wine

half a lemon

mash

4 potatoes

125ml extra virgin olive oil

Peel and boil the potatoes until soft, drain, then whisk by hand with the oil. Season to taste.

Allow 10 minutes for the steaming: the seafood are all steamed together over boiling water containing the fish bones, the shells from the prawns, and half a lemon. Steaming gives a level of simplicity that creates a simple and healthy dish while retaining all the natural flavours. Once all the ingredients are in the steaming basket over the boiling broth allow no more than 5 minutes for all the fish to be cooked. By this stage the mussels will have opened, the scallops will be plump, the fish just firm, and the prawns will have taken on a pinky orange colour.

Rest the steaming basket to one side while you create the sauce. To a hot saucepan add 250ml of the steaming broth, the white wine, and the six saffron stamen. Reduce the liquid by a third, then add the double cream. Reduce again by a third and remove from the heat. Remember; the sauce will continue to cook in its own heat, so if needed you can add some more broth to thin it down a little.

Assemble the dish using the mash as the base and lap the dish with the sauce. Serve immediately

Chiffonade of vegetables and shellfish flavoured with fresh truffle

serves 4

350g crab meat, white only
150g lobster meat cooked & sliced
12 langoustine tails
4 scallops
20g truffle
juice of 1 lemon
4 lemon wedges

truffle vinaigrette
50ml hazelnut oil
100ml arachide oil
100ml corn oil
1 clove garlic, crushed
1 bay leaf
few leaves thyme
a pinch rock salt
a pinch peppercorns
3g truffles, chopped

scallop marinade
50ml corn oil
1 clove garlic
10g root ginger, chopped
1 teaspoon chopped chives

vegetable noodles
80g swede, peeled
120g celeriac, peeled
80g carrots, peeled
60g leeks, cleaned & washed
40g courgettes, unpeeled

20g mange tout
40g beetroot.

2-3 days before needed boil all the vinaigrette ingredients except the truffles together in a pan for 15 minutes. Strain, then cool to around 70°C and add the truffles. Leave to cool in a sealed jar and store until required.

Steam the scallops to half cook them, them cut each into 4 slices. Place the slices in the corn oil with the garlic clove, ginger, and chopped chives, and leave to marinate for 6-8 hours.

Cut the vegetables into slices 1mm thick, then cut into 'noodle' strips 4cm long, and 1cm wide. Blanch in salted water or vegetable stock, then cool immediately to retain the crispness and freshness. Drain well. Blanch the mange tout and top and tail to match the vegetable 'noodles'. Season with salt and pepper and toss with a little truffle vinaigrette. Separate the two halves and add to the vegetables and toss. Cook and cut the beetroot into very fine strips, then set aside.

Separate the crab meat with your fingers and remove any shells. Season with salt, pepper, lemon juice and truffle vinaigrette. Set aside to mature the flavour. Sprinkle the lobster meat and lanngoustine tails with truffle vinaigrette.

Arrange the crab meat in a heap in the centre of the plate. Sprinkle the vegetables on top, retaining the 'haystack' shape. Place alternatively around the base slices of lobster and marinated scallops (4 per salad). Place the langoustine tails on top of the heap, facing in opposite directions and sliding downwards.

Arrange a slice of truffle on each scallop; cut two slices of truffle per salad into a julienne and sprinkle over the salad. Sprinkle the beetroot julienne 'randomly' over all the plate and spoon a little of the truffle vinaigrette mixed with scallop marinade around the edges. Serve.

DAVID CUDDIHY & MARK CONROY

KILLASHEE HOUSE HOTEL & VILLA SPA

County Kildare, Republic of Ireland

Mussel soup with saffron sprigs

serves 4

500g small mussels
80g onion, chopped
120g tomato, type "pandelote"
150g vermicelli
extra virgin olive oil
5g fennel, green leaves only
1 small bouquet garni
1 pinch saffron pistil
50g Emmental cheese

Peel and remove the seeds of the tomatoes, and cook slowly with the onion and bouquet garni in olive oil.

Wash the mussels (the best type for this dish are 'de bouchot') and remove the feet. Cover them in a pan with a litre of cold water and cook moderately, from time to time removing the opened mussels. Drain the cooking juice through a fine chinois and add them to the onion and tomato mixture, removing the bouquet garni. Bring the pan to the boil and add the saffron and salt if necessary. After the pan has been boiling for around 10 minutes, add the vermicelli broken into chunks and cook for a further 18 minutes. Meanwhile remove the mussels from their shells. Add these to the soup and cook for a final two minutes.

Serve with toasted baguette and the grated Emmental.

DIDIER GUSCHING
JEBEL ALI GOLF RESORT & SPA
Dubai, UAE

Ravioli with raw scampi, tomato filtering and Caciottina cheese

serves 4

ravioli
300g flat egg pasta
12 scampi

Caciottina cheese
500ml full cream milk
1 dessert spoon rennet

tomato
4 ripe tomatoes
small bunch basil
1 onion, chopped
1 clove garlic

olive oil
herbs for garnish

Warm the milk for the Caciottina, add the rennet and let it set. Add 50ml of previously boiled salted water, and drain the curd in special baskets for 4-5 hours.

Slice and flavour the tomatoes with salt, oil, basil, onion and garlic. Leave to macerate for 2-3 hours, then strain, preserving the filtered juices.

Spread out the pasta and cut out twelve 6cm squares. Divide the cleaned scampi onto the centre of each square and season with salt and pepper. Dampen the edges and fold the pasta into triangular ravioli, ensuring the edges are properly sealed.

To finish, cook the ravioli in boiling salted water for three minutes, then drain. Carefully arrange the ravioli in the serving plate and pour over the filtered tomato juice: place a round of cheese in the centre. Season the cheese with a little salt and complete with a thread of oil and herbs.

ANTONINO CANNAVACCIUOLO

VILLA CRESPI

Lake d'Orta, Italy

Egg noodle wrapped tiger prawns with exotic fruit tian

serves 4

12 tiger prawns peeled & deveined
300g fresh yellow egg noodles
vegetable oil for deep frying

fruit chaat
80g diced papaya
80g diced watermelon
80g diced avocado
80g diced pineapple
80g diced mango
8g fresh chopped mint leaves
40ml lime juice

pickled mango
2 ripe mangoes
1 green chilli, sliced
250ml syrup (125g sugar dissolved in 125ml boiling water)
1 pinch cumin powder
1 pinch turmeric powder
30ml white vinegar
30ml lime juice
2g mustard seeds
1 curry leaf

tamarind chutney
40g tamarind
40g jaggery (palm sugar)
160g sugar
2g chilli powder
2g pepper powder
2g black salt
1g cumin powder

garnish
10ml coconut milk
5g red chilli, sliced
5g mint leaves, chopped
10g rice vermicelli
20g black sesame seed
20g white sesame seed

Season the tiger prawns with salt and pepper, wrap in fresh yellow egg noodles and deep fry until golden. Set aside. Dice the chaat fruits. In a bowl, toss gently with the lime juice and fresh mint.

For the pickled mango, prepare the sugar syrup and add all the ingredients except the mango. Bring to the boil, then set aside. Peel and dice the mangoes into 1cm cubes, add to the spiced syrup, and leave to marinate for at least 30 minutes.

For the tamarind chutney, soak the tamarind in water until the pulp extracts. Add the remaining ingredients and cook until it a syrup consistency is reached, then strain and set aside.

Fry the rice vermicelli until crisp. Assemble the individual diced fruits in layers in a 2 inch ring mold on the plate, starting with the mango and finishing with the papaya. Position 3 prawns in a triangle shape against the fruit tian. Arrange tamarind chutney, pickled mango, and the garnishes of coconut milk, sesame seeds, red chili and fresh mint around the fruit tian. Garnish the top with the crispy rice noodle vermicelli and serve immediately.

WOLFGANG EBERLE
DUSIT DUBAI
Dubai, United Arab Emirates

Crispy fried dragon prawns with mandarin orange coriander salsa, longan filled with prawn and chilli salsa on lime jelly

serves 4

crispy dragon prawn

8 fresh prawns,
cleaned & de-veined

100g prawn crackers, crumbled

1 egg

2 tablespoons potato starch

1 pinch chilli powder

2 tablespoons cake flour
(available from Asian stores)

orange coriander dressing

80ml freshly squeezed orange juice

100g orange segments,
chopped into small dice

2 tablespoons coriander oil

sweet vinegar sauce

100ml black vinegar

100ml water and sugar solution
boiled to a syrup

1 tablespoon ginger juice

chilli salsa

10g each green, yellow, and red
capsicum, chopped into small dice

10g red onion,
chopped into small dice

2 tablespoons Thai sweet chilli sauce

cucumber lime jelly

50g cucumber
trimmed to eight thick slices 2.5cm
square with hollow centres

100ml lime juice

5 gelatine leaves
soaked in a little water

prawn filled longan

2 fresh prawns,
cleaned & de-veined

8 longans, peeled & cleaned

garnish

2 sticks celery
cut into desired shape for garnish

4 sprigs coriander leaf

Prepare the orange and coriander dressing by mixing all the ingredients together. Season with salt to taste and reserve for use later. Do the same for the sweet vinegar sauce. Mix the peppers and onion with the chilli sauce for the chilli salsa.

For the cucumber lime jelly, dissolve the soaked gelatine in the lime juice by gently warming both together in a pan. Dip the cucumber cubes in the lime jelly and leave to one side to cool and set.

Gently poach the prawns for the filled longan in softly boiling seasoned water until cooked, then remove from the pan to drain and cool. Chop the prawns into a dice small enough to fill the longan fruit: season. Fill the longans with the prawn mix

Set the fryer temperature to 180°C. Combine the egg, potato starch, chilli powder and cake flour for the crispy dragon prawns until well mixed with no lumps. Dip the prawns in the batter, then coat with the cracked prawn crackers. Deep fry in hot oil until crispy, then drain off excess oil and season with salt to taste.

When ready, place the warm prawns in the centre of the plate. Arrange filled longans on cucumber squares to one side, with a teaspoon of chilli salsa on each longan. Dress the prawns with a little vineger dressing; pour orange sauce around the outside. Garnish with celery and coriander leaf as desired.

LEONG CHEE YENG : ZHENG HE'S RESTAURANT, MINA A' SALAM
MADINAT JUMEIRAH, THE ARABIAN RESORT – DUBAI
Dubai, United Arab Emirates

Shrimp Chanjie with a roasted coconut dip

FASHAD MOHAMMED

FORT YOUNG HOTEL

Roseau, Dominica

serves 4

20 extra large shrimps,
peeled, deveined, tail on
240ml split peas, ground
1 teaspoon garlic, minced
1 teaspoon turmeric powder
1 teaspoon baking powder
6 tablespoons flour
250ml water
250ml oil for frying

coconut dip
1 dry coconut kernel
2 cloves garlic, roasted & minced
2 chilli peppers, finely chopped
2 teaspoons cilantro, chopped
4 tablespoons mayonnaise

Slowly roast the coconut on a charbroiler until browned, then shred on a grater or finely mince. Combine with the remaining ingredients for the dip and set aside.

Coat the shrimps with flour and store in the fridge. Combine the remaining flour with the rest of the ingredients except the oil, seasoned with a little salt and pepper, to form a batter: Holding the tail, dip each shrimp individually in the batter and fry until brown. Drain on paper towels to absorb any excess oil. Serve with the coconut dip, accompanied by rice or potato.

Seared crayfish and tiger prawn
with spiced coconut curry cream

serves 4

4 x 200g crayfish
8 x 60g tiger prawns with shells
2 tablespoons butter

marinade
4 tablespoons lime juice
1 teaspoon salt
half a teaspoon black pepper

accompanying vegetables
100g lotus roots
100g snake gourd
2 garlic cloves, chopped
half a teaspoon salt
2 tablespoons butter

spiced coconut curry cream
4 garlic cloves, chopped
2 large onions, chopped
2 tomatoes, chopped
2 sprigs curry leaves
10cm rampe (pandanus) leaf
4 tablespoons curry powder
2 teaspoons chilli powder
2 teaspoons turmeric powder
5g cinnamon stick
3 cloves
2 cardamom
500ml coconut milk
2 tablespoon corn oil
2 teaspoons salt

cumin vegetable rice
200g basmati rice
5g cumin seeds
1 clove garlic, chopped
half a teaspoon turmeric powder
20g bell peppers, small dice
20g tomatoes, small dice
1 onion, chopped
20g carrot, small dice
500ml vegetable stock
2 teaspoons salt
25g ghee

To prepare the crayfish remove the head and break the tail section at each shell joint into segments. De-vein the tiger prawns. Marinade the crayfish and prawns in the lime juice, salt and black pepper for an hour. To cook, sear the crayfish and tiger prawns in hot butter.

For the curry cream, heat the oil in a pan and sauté the garlic, onions and tomato with the curry leaf and rampe, then add the spices. Gradually stir in the coconut milk. Bring the sauce to the boil, then reduce the heat and simmer for 6-7 minutes. Strain the curry cream then season with salt.

Prepare the cumin vegetable rice by cooking the cumin in ghee for two minutes, then add the garlic, turmeric powder and other vegetables. Sauté for a short while then mix in the washed basmati rice, stir the mixture till the rice heats, then add the vegetable stock, cover with a lid and cook for 15 minutes.

Thinly slice the lotus roots and snake gourd and heat the butter in a pan, Sauté the garlic then add the lotus roots and snake gourd and cook for four minutes, seasoning with salt.

To serve arrange the crayfish and tiger prawns with a timbale of cumin vegetable rice. Place the sautéd lotus roots and snake gourd, heat the curry cream and ensure a generous serving.

NIHAL SENANAYAKE

LIGHTHOUSE HOTEL & SPA

Galle, Sri Lanka

Rosette of tiger shrimp with sesame butter

serves 4

16 tiger shrimp (approx 1kg)
half a mango
quarter of a cantaloupe
quarter of a papaya
half an avocado
mixed baby salad greens
zest of half an orange
zest of half a lemon
2 teaspoons sesame seeds
juice of 1 lemon

sesame butter

50g shallots, finely chopped
2 tablespoons white vinegar
4 tablespoons dry white wine
2 tablespoons fresh cream
200g of butter, cut in pieces
2 tablespoons sesame oil

Lightly steam the shrimp, then remove their shells and cut them in half lengthways. Cut the mango, papaya, cantaloupe and avocado into fine strips and sprinkle with lemon juice. Blanch the julienne orange and lemon zests and set aside.

Bring the shallots, vinegar and white wine to the boil and let the liquid reduce almost completely. Add the cream, reduce the heat, and whisk in the butter piece by piece, then add the sesame oil.

Make a bed of salad greens in the centre of each serving plate. Top with the sliced fruit, a grinding of pepper and 8 shrimp halves in the form of a rosette. Dress with the sesame butter and sprinkle with the julienne zests and sesame seeds.

PATRICK LANNES
LE ROYAL MERIDIEN BEACH RESORT & SPA
Dubai, United Arab Emirates

34

Seared scallops, sweet potato, pineapple, coconut and asian spiced foam

serves 4

sweet potato purée
500g large sweet potatoes
250g unsalted butter, softened

12 large scallops
25g unsalted butter
juice of half a lemon
fresh coconut shavings
(keep the coconut milk for the foam)

pineapple crisps
1 medium pineapple
500ml sugar stock syrup

curry foam
50g diced shallots
1 clove garlic, crushed
spices for curry powder
(pinch of turmeric, garam masala,
ground cumin, coriander seed,
cardamom seed and chilli powder.)

sultanas
50g sultanas
300ml red wine
1 cinnamon stick

olive oil
175g cooked large leaf spinach
chervil or coriander leaves for garnish

900ml fish stock
300ml double cream

Prepare the dried pineapple crisps and sultanas a day in advance. Top and tail the pineapple and trim the sides to remove the tough skin. Set a gravity slicing machine as thin as possible and slice the pineapple whole to give perfect round thin slices. Dip each slice into the stock syrup and shake off any surplus syrup, then place on a non stick mat and dry in a low oven for 4 hours at 100°C. Remove from the oven and cut the rounds in half before they cool, then allow to cool. The discs should crisp: if not continue drying in the oven.

For the sultanas soaked in red wine, add the red wine and cinnamon stick to the stock syrup from the pineapple in a saucepan. Bring to the boil and reduce by half, then add the sultanas. Remove from the heat and allow to cool, leaving the sultanas to marinate in the syrup. Store when cooled ready for use.

For the sweet potato purée, wrap the sweet potatoes in their skins in tin foil and bake in the oven at 170°C until soft, then take out of the oven and remove the skin whilst still hot. Place into a blender. Add the softened butter and blend to a silky smooth purée. Season to taste and keep warm ready for use.

To prepare the curry foam sweat the shallots and garlic without colour with a little oil. Add a teaspoon of the curry spice mix and sweat again without colour for 5 minutes. Add the fish stock and reduce by half. Add the cream and coconut milk then reduce slightly. Keep the sauce loose, ready to foam with a hand blender. Pass through double thick muslin, correct the seasoning to taste and keep warm to one side.

When ready, cook the seasoned scallops presentation side first in a little oil for a minute to a minute and a half until they're a nice golden brown. Add the butter and lemon juice, turn the scallops over and remove the pan from the heat. Baste the scallops with the cooking liquor, then let the heat from the pan carry on cooking the scallops for a further minute. Once cooked, warm and season the spinach and arrange all the ingredients onto plates. Foam the sauce with a hand blender and present using your imagination (and with the picture as reference).

DAREN BALE
THE ELMS HOTEL AND RESTAURANT
Worcestershire, England

Panaché of roasted scallops and foie gras, sauce Sauternes

IAN MCNAUGHT

THE ROMAN CAMP HOTEL

Perthshire, Scotland

For the chutney, melt the butter in a pan, add the diced shallot and cook for 2 minutes without colour. Add all the other ingredients except the sugar and cook slowly until all the moisture has gone, then transfer the mix to a blender, add the sugar, and purée. Check the seasoning and set aside.

To prepare the sauce, sweat the shallots and mushrooms in 50g butter until softened without colour, then add the Sauternes and bring the pan to the boil. Reduce by half, then add the chicken stock and bring to the boil and reduce by half again. Add the scallop stock, bring to the boil, and reduce by half. Finally add the cream and bring to the boil, then simmer for 5 minutes, season, and pass the sauce through a sieve into a clean pan.

To serve, cut the baby beetroot in half, season, and warm up in a knob of butter with a tablespoon of chicken stock. Cut the baby leeks into two, season, and warm up in a knob of butter with 2 tablespoons of chicken stock. Melt a knob of butter, add 2 tablespoons of chicken stock, add the diced courgette and rocket leaves and cook and season.

Cut the scallops in half. Heat up 2 non-stick pans, season the scallops and cook for about 30 seconds each side, depending on the thickness. Season and cook the foie gras on both sides, keeping it nice and pink in the middle. Gently warm the Sauternes sauce and chutney.

Place three scallop halves overlapping on one side of each of 4 heated plates. Criss-cross 6 pieces of baby leek down the centre of the plate, with the rocket and diced courgette and baby beetroot the other side of the leeks. Top with the foie gras and a quenelle of chutney, pour sauce around, and serve.

serves 4

6 extra large diver caught scallops
4 x 50g escalopes of foie gras
6 baby beetroot, cooked & peeled
12 baby leeks, blanched
1 courgette, finely diced
200g small rocket leaves
50g butter
5 tablespoons chicken stock

fig & mango chutney
50g butter
2 shallots diced
10 dried figs
50ml apple juice
15ml balsamic vinegar
15ml sherry vinegar
1 teaspoon Dijon mustard
1 clove garlic, crushed
50g raisins
60g caster sugar

sauce Sauternes
2 shallots, finely sliced
4 button mushrooms, finely sliced
50g unsalted butter
150ml Sauternes
100 ml chicken stock
100ml scallop stock
150 ml double cream

Lobster escabèche
with candied olives and black olive emulsion

serves 4

1kg live Atlantic lobster
1 red pepper, liquidised
300g cherry tomatoes,
blanched, refreshed & peeled
200g dried black olives
100ml sugar syrup
1 egg,
simmered in the shell for 3 minutes
200ml chicken stock
1 teaspoon parsley, chopped
300g Jerusalem artichokes, peeled
a dash double cream

paprika oil
2 cloves garlic, crushed
2 sprigs thyme
1 bay leaf
1 teaspoon ground paprika
30ml sherry vinegar

butter
olive oil

Begin a day in advance by preparing the paprika oil for the lobsters. Heat the garlic, thyme and bay leaf in a little olive oil until lightly toasted, then add the smoked paprika and sherry vinegar and adjust the seasoning. Finally add another 30ml of olive oil and gently warm, then set aside for 24 hours to infuse.

On a silicon baking sheet, dry out the red pepper juice in a very low oven until it becomes a sheet like paper.

Poach half the dried olives in the syrup (50g sugar dissolved in 50ml water) for 10 minutes. Remove the olives from the liquid, place on a parchment lined baking sheet, and dry in a very low oven until slightly crunchy. Poach the remaining half of the olives in the chicken stock then transfer to the blender. Peel and add the egg, then with the blender on add 25g of butter and 20ml of olive oil in a steady stream. Adjust the seasoning.

Poach the lobster for 3 minutes in salted simmering water, then plunge into iced water to stop the cooking. Remove the claw meat, cut the tails in half lengthways, clean out the intestinal tract, and reserve the meat and tails.

Peel the Jerusalem artichokes and cook in a single layer, with just enough water to cover them and 15g of butter. Adjust the seasoning, then purée the cooked artichokes with a dash of cream and 25g of butter until smooth.

When ready, heat up and strain the paprika oil. Use the oil to cook the lobster meat for about 3 minutes until done. Separately warm the tomatoes through without cooking them, then add the candied olives and chopped parsley. Reheat the artichoke purée.

Plate the dish by spooning the artichoke purée onto the plate, followed by the tomato mixture and the lobster. Give the sauce a last quick spin in the blender, and use only the froth on top. Garnish with strip of the red pepper 'paper'.

MICHAEL A GOODMAN : NAPA, AL QASR
MADINAT JUMEIRAH, THE ARABIAN RESORT – DUBAI
Dubai, United Arab Emirates

Butter poached lobster
with cardamom, coriander and basmati rice

JOHN T WILLIAMS
THE RITZ LONDON
London, England

Blanch the lobsters in boiling water for 20 seconds to free the flesh from the carcass. Break off and carry on cooking the claws for a full 2 minutes, then refresh in iced water. Break the head from the body then crack the tail to remove the tail meat from the shell. Repeat with the claws and knuckle. Clean the head of any grey matter and reserve the coral to use in the sauce later.

Chop the shell into small equal pieces. Heat a heavy sauce pan and sauté the shell in the butter until it roasts lightly and becomes red in colour. Add the onion and carrot and sweat for approximately 10 minutes, then add the celeriac, fennel, ginger, cardamom and coriander and cook slowly to allow the perfume to develop. Flambé with the brandy, allowing the alcohol to totally vaporise, and reduce the liquid to a fine glaze.

Add the lobster and chicken stocks and slowly reduce by half. Add the cream, bring to the boil slowly and simmer very gently for 10 minutes. Season and pass through a fine chinois, and finish by whisking in the coral which has been passed through a sieve. This must be done away from the heat or it will curdle the sauce. Reserve.

To prepare the basmati wash the rice several times in running water if required, then leave to soak for 20 minutes. Finely dice the onion, garlic and ginger. Heat the butter in a pan over a medium heat, add the onion, and cook for a couple of minutes before adding the other ingredients. When they are releasing their perfume add the rice, a little sea salt, and 600ml of water. Bring the pan to the boil, cover with a tight fitting lid and braise in the oven or cook gently on top of the stove for approximately 18 minutes. Once cooked run a fork through the rice just before serving: it should be light, fluffy, and full of flavour.

Bring the clarified butter up to temperature about 65°C and very slowly poach the lobster meat for 5 minutes, then lift out and drain on kitchen paper. Place a ring of basmati rice in the centre of the plate and rest the lobster portions on top. Foam the cardamom sauce with a Bamix mixer and pour generously over the lobster, finishing with a few leaves of coriander and the broad beans.

serves 4

4x 500g British lobsters
500g clarified butter
quarter of a bunch fresh coriander

100g butter
40g onions, diced
40g carrots, diced
40g celeriac, diced
40g fennel, diced
30g root ginger
6-8 cardamom pods
10 coriander seeds
50g broad beans
40ml brandy
250 ml lobster stock
125 ml chicken stock
25ml double cream

basmati rice

450ml basmati rice
40g chopped onion
2 cloves garlic
25g root ginger
2 cardamom pods
10 coriander seeds, fresh if possible
half a fresh bayleaf
50g butter

Spring roll of lemon sole with salmon mousse, sautéed scallops and a red pepper and tomato dressing

serves 4

2 lemon sole fillets
2 spring roll wrappers
12 large basil leaves
vegetable oil for frying
12 large king scallops, roe removed

egg wash
4 egg yolks & a little water

mousse
100g salmon fillet, skinned & pin boned
1 whole egg
150ml double cream

tomato and red pepper dressing
6 plum tomatoes, finely chopped
2 red peppers,
deseeded & chopped into quarters
4 shallots, chopped
1 clove garlic, chopped
25ml white wine
1 bay leaf
600ml vegetable stock
100ml olive oil

garnish
lettuce leaves
walnut oil
1 roasted red pepper,
skinned & finely chopped
12 sprigs chervil

To make the dressing sweat the shallots, garlic and bay leaf off without colour in a pan. Add the pepper and the chopped tomato and keep cooking until the tomatoes start to go soft, then add all the remaining dressing ingredients except the olive oil. Simmer until the liquid has reduced by a third, then liquidise and pass through a sieve. When cool whisk in the olive oil and set aside.

For the mousse, chill the uncooked salmon in a food processor bowl for 10 minutes in the freezer, then add a good pinch of salt and blend until smooth. Add the egg and continue to blend until it is incorporated into the salmon. Finally blend in the cream.

Next place one lemon sole fillet between two pieces of cling film (large enough to cover the fillet) and batten out using a meat hammer or rolling pin. Repeat with the second fillet. Spread a smooth layer of salmon mousse on top of each fillet with a row of basil leaves along one edge. Roll the fillet up to form a Swiss roll, smearing a little mousse on the outside of the roll to help it stay together when cooked. Place the roll on an egg-washed spring roll wrapper and roll it neatly to form a fat cigar shape.

Deep fry the spring roll at 170°C for 5 minutes until golden brown. When cooked, drain and leave to one side. Next sear the scallops in a hot pan in a little oil for 10-15 seconds on each side.

To assemble the dish, slice the spring roll in half diagonally and place upright on an assortment of lettuce leaves dressed with walnut oil. Place three scallops around the spring roll and top each scallop with a tiny pile of roasted red peppers: drizzle with the tomato and red pepper dressing. Garnish the dish with sprigs of chervil.

GARY BUXTON
THE GIBBON BRIDGE HOTEL
Lancashire, England

Turbot squares on a seafood and asparagus bed

serves 4

500g turbot fillet
12 pieces baby squid
8 green asparagus spears
4 'carabinero' shrimps
150g nori seaweed, crispy fried
butter
vegetable oil for deep frying
olive oil

sauce
1 medium lobster
2 shallots
1 medium onion
2 cloves garlic, sliced
200g tomatoes, chopped
1 tablespoon tomato paste
500ml lobster (or fish) stock
I bunch fresh dill, chopped

Extract the lobster meat, removing and reserving the pale green tomalley and the orange roe. Melt a knob of butter in a saucepan and sauté the shallots and onion until lightly browned. Add the lobster meat and shells, garlic, tomatoes, and tomato paste to the saucepan and sauté for 5 minutes. Add 25g or so of flour and stir well to make a roux. Add the stock a third at a time, stirring continually. When all the stock has been used add the dill and simmer for 20 minutes, stirring frequently. Season with salt and pepper to taste, then strain through a fine chinois and keep warm.

Brush the baby squid, shrimp and asparagus with oil and grill under a moderate heat, turning occasionally, until the squid is golden brown all over and the shrimp turns red: do not let the squid cook too quickly. Keep everything warm. Heat the vegetable oil in a pan until it is hazy but not smoking: tip the nori seaweed and fry in the oil for about 2 minutes until it is crisp and pale.

Grill the turbot fillet, white skin side up, under a moderately high heat for 5 minutes, then turn the fish and cook the other side for 5 minutes. Place the turbot on a bed of asparagus and spoon the sauce onto the plate around the fish. Arrange squid and shrimp on top of the fillet, and complete the plate with crispy nori between the squid.

BENITO GONZÁLEZ PÉREZ

GRAN MELIA SALINAS - THE GARDEN VILLAS
Canary Islands, Spain

Roast fillet of halibut, saffron potatoes, smoked haddock chowder foam

serves 4

4 x 180g halibut suprêmes
from a large fish
4 heads baby bok choi

sauce
1 shallot, finely diced
1 clove garlic, crushed
2 sprigs thyme
150g smoked haddock off cuts
1 shot brandy
300ml fish stock
100ml cream
150ml milk
150g butter

vegetable garnish
2 jumbo potatoes, peeled
half a teaspoon saffron

chowder
1 shallot, finely diced
12 clams
12 mussels
25ml white wine
50g cubed smoked bacon
50g peeled prawns
50g cooked peas
1 teaspoon mixed chopped herbs

garnish
deep fried herbs
choux paste
poppy seeds

Cut the potatoes into 6 thick slices, then cut out a 3cm circle from each with a cookie cutter; keep some of the trimmings for the sauce. Place the discs in a pan of cold water with the saffron and season well, bring to the boil and simmer until cooked

To prepare the sauce, sweat off the shallot, garlic, thyme and smoked fish trimmings in a sauce pan, then add the brandy and fish stock and reduce by half. Blend this with a stick blender and pass through a chinois back into a clean pan, then add the cream and milk and keep warm, but do not boil

For the chowder, sweat off the shallot, add the clams and mussels and white wine and cover for 2 minutes, then add the smoked bacon and cook for 2 further minutes. Finally add the prawns, peas and herbs and leave under lights to keep warm

Season the fish well and allow them to stand for 5 minutes, then pat the skin side with kitchen paper to absorb the extra moisture. Place the fish skin side down in a hot non-stick pan and cook until the skin is browned and crispy, then turn the fish over, turn down the heat, and allow the fish to cook through on the low heat. When cooked place in a warm place to rest

Trim and colour the bok choi in the fish pan with a little extra butter, then place on a tray and roast for a few minutes at 150°C until the white ends are soft

To assemble place three saffron potatoes around the centre of each plate with the bok choi in the middle. Spread the chowder evenly around the potatoes in a ring, and place a piece of haddock on top of the bok choi. Put the plates under a warm grill while you finish the sauce

Heat up the sauce without letting it boil, then take off the heat and put in the butter, in cubes. While the butter is melting froth up the sauce with a stick blender. Spoon just the foam off the top of the sauce over the chowder, top the fish with deep fried herbs and a poppy seed choux tuille, and serve immediately.

SIMON GREEN

PENDLEY MANOR HOTEL

Hertfordshire, England

Sole and crab cake, sauce Nantaise

serves 4

300g Dover sole fillet,
cooked & diced

300g white crab meat

60g carrot, diced & blanched

20g chopped chervil

100g mayonnaise

200g fresh white breadcrumbs

2 eggs for wash

80g flour

2 vine plum tomatoes

4 sprigs chervil

sauce

120ml white wine

120ml white wine vinegar

120g shallots, diced

100g butter unsalted

juice of half a lemon

Blanch and cut the tomatoes into quarters, remove all the seeds and cut the flesh into small diamonds.

Gently fold the Dover sole, white crab meat, carrot, chervil and mayonnaise together. Season well, and with a 10cm diameter ring mould gently into four cakes about 2cm thick. Cover the cakes with film and place in the fridge for at least 30 minutes.

Sprinkle flour on both sides of the cake, brush with egg wash and coat with the fresh breadcrumbs. Panfry the crab cake in clarified butter using a non stick frying pan. When golden browned on all sides remove the cakes and keep warm.

For the sauce, slowly reduce the shallots, white wine, and vinegar together in a pan to a syrup consistency. Gently emulsify the unsalted butter in the reduction and season with lemon juice to make a sharp Nantaise sauce.

Serve garnished with the tomato diamonds and sprigs of chervil.

JÉRÔME PONCHELLE
WILTONS RESTAURANT
London, England

Sumac marinated salmon and crab
with loomi dressing and soft herbs

serves 4

500g salmon fillet
250g picked crab claw meat

marinade
2 stalks lemongrass
100g fine sugar
100g sea salt
20g mixed peppercorns
30g sumac powder

dressing
60ml lime juice
20g fine sugar
1 grated loomi (dried lime)
5g potato starch or arrowroot
25ml extra virgin olive oil
5ml good soy sauce

garnish
10g picked coriander leaf
15g very finely chopped chives
4 finely sliced young spring onions
10g picked chervil
1 head curly endive

Sumac powder is brilliant red in color and frequently used in dishes throughout the Middle East. Made from the dried and ground berries of the sumac plant, it gives a slightly sour taste with citrus overtones. This is a dish I created with Anton Mosimann when I was Executive Chef for him in London, given a Middle Eastern twist for visitors of Al Maha to enjoy.

For the marinated salmon, finely slice then blend the lemongrass in a food processor to break down the fibres as much as possible. Mix together with the sugar, salt, milled pepper and sumac powder and completely smother the salmon fillet in the mixture, including the underside. Leave for 18-24 hours to marinate, then gently rinse the mixture off the salmon with fresh water.

In a pot, bring the lime juice, sugar and dried loomi to the boil. Blend the starch with a little cold water and whisk into the boiling sauce until a mayonnaise consistency has formed, then remove from the heat. Pass through a sieve and, whilst still warm, slowly whisk in the extra virgin olive oil until the sauce gives off a shiny texture. Finally, finish the dressing with a dash of soy sauce to taste.

Slice the salmon thinly and carefully arrange in a circle on the plate. Cover the salmon generously with the prepared crab meat and season with a little more sumac powder, then arrange the soft leaves and herbs over the top of the crab and dress the salad liberally with the lime dressing. Serve immediately.

JAMES WEBSTER

AL MAHA DESERT RESORT

Dubai, UAE

Trio of marinated Scottish salmon
with cucumber, crème fraîche and caviar

Marinate the salmon at least 24 hours before it is required. Mix the salt, sugar and lime zest together. Lay the salmon fillet skin down on aluminium foil and sprinkle with the Pernod. Cover the salmon with the salt mixture, wrap the fish in the foil and refrigerate for 24 hours. After 24 hours remove from the foil and gently wash the salmon under cold running water to remove all the salt mix. Portion the salmon into the specified sizes.

For the sushi rolls, bring the rice, rice wine and vinegar with 165ml water to the boil in a pan and simmer with the lid on for 10 minutes. Remove from the heat and leave to stand for a further 15-20 minutes without removing the lid. Lay out the Nori sheet, spread some of the rice over three quarters of the paper and lay the salmon and cucumber batons through the middle. Roll the sushi into a tight roll, trying to keep the salmon and cucumber towards the middle of the roll (It is easier to roll if you do this directly on cling film or a sushi mat). Cover with cling film and refrigerate.

For the cucumber rolls, peel the cucumber and slice lengthways very thinly on a mandolin or meat slicer. Place the marinated salmon in the middle, lay a few pea shoots over the top and roll the cucumber to form a loose roll. Gently mix the crème fraîche and lime juice, seasoning to taste with salt and pepper.

For the grilled salmon mix the mustard and honey together, spread a small amount on top of the salmon and place on a tray ready to go under the grill. Peel and cut the mango into a small dice; repeat with the red onion and mix the two together with the chopped coriander and rice wine vinegar.

To assemble the dish gently cut the sushi roll on an angle and stand upright on the plate. Place a circle of crème fraîche in the middle of the plate with the cucumber roll on top and garnish with caviar and a few extra pea shoots. Warm the salmon with mustard under the grill for a few minutes, then place the mango salsa on the plate and rest the grilled salmon on top.

serves 4

marinated salmon

800g salmon fillet
180g salt
250g sugar
3 tablespoons Pernod
zest from 1 lime
(save the juice for later)

sushi rolls

2 strips marinated salmon
approx 1.5cm x 1.5cm x 15cm
125g sushi rice
2 tablespoons rice wine
2 tablespoons rice wine vinegar
2 sushi nori sheets
half a cucumber cut to the same
size as the salmon strips

cucumber roll

4 pieces marinated salmon
approx 2cm x 2cm x 5cm
half a cucumber
1 punnet pea shoots
6 tablespoons crème fraîche
juice of 1 lime
1x 30g tin sevruga caviar

grilled salmon

4 pieces marinated salmon
approx 6cm square
2 tablespoon grain mustard
2 tablespoon honey
1 mango
half a red onion
small bunch coriander
1 tablespoon rice wine vinegar

STEVEN TITMAN

SUMMER LODGE COUNTRY HOUSE HOTEL, RESTAURANT & SPA

Dorset, England

Fillet of wild salmon freshly smoked on turf
with a cream sauce of fresh tarragon

serves 4

4x 130-150g portions wild salmon,
filleted skinned & pin boned

fresh turf & smoking powder/dust
(fine smoking wood chips)

sauce:

200g fish stock

1 shallot, peeled & finely diced

150g white wine

100g fresh cream

1 small bunch of fresh tarragon,
washed & sliced

20g finest tarragon vinegar

50g fresh cream, whipped

garnish

12 small potatoes, neatly shaped
(optional), steamed

2 medium sized carrots, peeled

1 leek, washed

1 medium courgette, washed

50g butter

4 sprigs of tarragon

For the sauce, reduce the fish stock with the white wine and shallots by half. Add the fresh cream and reduce by again by two thirds. Strain the sauce through a fine sieve and keep warm.

Cut the carrots, courgette and leeks into fine strips and sweat in the butter until soft. Season to taste and keep hot. Toss the steamed potatoes in a little butter, season to taste, and keep hot.

Season each fish portion with salt and pepper. Place a very small amount of smoking powder/dust or wood chips with a pea-sized piece of turf – or peat if available – at the bottom of a domestic smoker: this can be purchased in a fishing tackle shop. The amount of powder/dust and turf depends on personal taste and the size of the smoker, as well as the intensity of heat: do a test smoking starting with small quantities of chips and increase as required. Place the salmon fillets on the smoking grid in the smoker, and close the lid. Place the smoker on a the hob and smoke for 5-10 minutes until the fish is cooked medium to taste. The cooking time will vary depending on the heat source and type of smoker, but the fish should have only a very mild taste of smoke to complement the flavour of the salmon.

To finish the sauce, return to the heat, add the vinegar and tarragon, fold in the whipped cream and adjust the seasoning. Present the hot salmon on a bed of vegetable julienne, pour a little sauce around the salmon and garnish with tossed steamed potatoes and a sprig of fresh tarragon. Serve immediately.

STEFAN MATZ
ASHFORD CASTLE
County Mayo, Republic of Ireland

Roasted wild Scottish salmon
with a shellfish, chorizo and white bean cassoulet

serves 4

cassoulet

250g surf clams
250g mussels, de-bearded
2 banana shallots
60g butter
200ml white wine
200g Spanish white beans
(soaked overnight in 2 litres of
water then drained)
3 chorizo sausage (the raw type)
500ml double cream

salmon

4 x160g salmon fillets
25ml olive oil
30g butter

squid

4 baby squid tubes, cleaned
10ml olive oil
1 tablespoon chopped chives

For the cassoulet, first slice and sweat one of the shallots in half the butter until soft, then add first the washed clams, then the wine. Cover with a tight fitting lid and steam for one to two minutes over a fierce heat. Pour the contents of the pan into a sieve over a bowl to catch all the juices. Pick out the clam meat, discard the shells, and place the meat in the fridge for later Repeat the same process for the mussels.

In a large heavy based pan add the beans, the cooking liquor from the shellfish, and the cream and cook slowly on a gentle heat for about 45 minutes until the beans are tender. Bake the chorizo in the oven until firm, then dice and add to the cooked beans along with any oil from the cooking. Finally add the mussels and clams to the hot beans.

Season the salmon. Heat the oil in a hot non-stick pan, adding the salmon skin side down when good and hot. Cook for 1-2 minutes, then add the butter: as it melts, baste the salmon. Remove from the heat and turn the fish over to let the residual heat finish the cooking.

Cut the squid into fine rings. Heat the oil in a non-stick pan. Season the squid and quickly fry for 1 minute. Drain on paper towels and sprinkle with the chopped chives.

To serve, place 2 tablespoons of the beans in the centre of a plate. Sit the salmon on top and balance some of the squid on top of the salmon. Serve immediately.

PAUL HART
CRINGLETIE HOUSE
Peebles, Scotland

Yellowfin tuna ceviche with homegrown coconut water, West Indian Scotch Bonnet chillies and organic herbs

serves 8 as starter

marinade

3 tablespoons
white balsamic vinegar

75ml lime juice

75ml lemon juice

2 tablespoons fish sauce

2 tablespoons honey

2 tablespoons coconut water
(from the fresh coconut)

1 tablespoon Scotch bonnet
pepper, minced fine (adjust to taste)

400g yellowfin tuna, diced

150ml extra virgin olive oil

3 teaspoons lemon zest

100g toasted coconut flakes

50g cilantro, roughly chopped

2 tablespoons mint,
roughly chopped

2 tablespoons tarragon

to serve

4 coconuts, split in half

16 garlic chives for garnish

half a cup toasted coconut, chilled

1 tablespoon lemon zest

sea salt as needed (large crystals)

4 key limes, cut in half & seeded

8 bowls filled with crushed ice

To make the marinade, combine the citrus juices, vinegar, fish sauce, honey, coconut water, and pepper in a bowl and mix well. Taste and adjust the seasoning as needed with salt, pepper, and additional citrus juices.

Just before serving, mix the fish with the olive oil, the marinade and the chopped herbs. Taste and adjust seasoning as needed.

To plate, fill the coconut halves with the ceviche and place in the bowls of ice. Top with the sea salt and decorate with the toasted coconut, chives and lemon zest. Accompany with key limes

DANIEL ORR & CHRISTOPHER HEATH

CUISINART RESORT & SPA

Anguilla, British West Indies

Baked tuna fish with Mediterranean herbs and a fish gravy with saffron pistils

Coat the tuna fillets in chopped mixed herbs and fry in a non stick frying pan with a little extra virgin olive oil until golden. Finish cooking in the oven at 170°C for 6 minutes.

Heat the fish stock with the shallots, add the saffron pistils, and cook until the gravy thickens. Whisk the gravy with a little extra virgin olive oil.

Pour the gravy onto the plate and fan slices of tuna over it. Decorate the dish with the steamed mixed vegetables and the remaining aromatic herbs.

serves 4

480g fresh tuna fish fillets
aromatic herbs: thyme, mint, oregano, rosemary & marjoram
300ml fish stock
40g shallots, chopped
15 saffron pistils
extra virgin olive oil

400g mixed vegetables, steamed

GIUSEPPE ARGENTINO
GROTTA GIUSTI NATURAL SPA RESORT
Tuscany, Italy

Grilled pepper tuna with Portobello and tomato ragout, organic fresh greens, coriander jus

Preparation time 20 minutes

serves 4

4 x 180g fillets yellow fin tuna
4 Portobello mushroom
4 medium tomatoes
2 tablespoons cracked black pepper
2 tablespoons purple basil leaf

3 tablespoons coriander leaf
2 tablespoons arugula leaves
2 tablespoons parsley
3 tablespoons olive oil
1 clove garlic

Ask your fishmonger to prepare four of the freshest tuna steaks. Using the tuna at the peak of its freshness, roll each steak in cracked peppercorns and reserve to one side.

Peel, wash, and cut the Portobello mushroom into cubes. Sautée the mushrooms gently in olive oil. Meanwhile, peel and de-seed the tomatoes, cut into cubes and add to the mushrooms. Add fresh basil, salt and pepper. Reserve to one side.

To make the coriander jus blanch half the coriander, basil and parsley in boiling water for 5 seconds then cool in ice water. Mix in the blender with garlic and olive oil, adding salt and pepper to taste. Wash and dry the remaining green leaves then mix them together and reserve to one side.

Heat a non-stick pan until hot, add the tuna steak and pan sear it for 20 seconds on all sides. The outer flesh should be browned with the inner core rare.

To serve, arrange the Portobello mushroom and tomato mixture in the centre of the plate. Slice the tuna steak and place on top. Finally, top off with the mixed greens and drizzle the coriander jus around.

DANIEL ECHASSERIAU
THE BODYHOLIDAY LESPORT
Castries, St Lucia

Fillet of red mullet on a pea risotto
with lemon and thyme Mascarpone

serves 4

4 x180g fillets of red mullet
50ml olive oil

pea stock
300g peas
1 litre vegetable stock
2 shallots, finely chopped

for the risotto
2 shallots, finely chopped
1 clove garlic, crushed
100g unsalted butter
225g Carnaroli rice
40g shelled broad beans
40g peas

garnish
4 finely sliced pieces of lemon
4 basil leaves deep fried
100g Mascarpone
grated zest of 1 lemon
1 teaspoon thyme leaves

Dust the lemon slices for garnish in icing sugar, then dry them in the oven at 100°C for three hours. Combine the Mascarpone with the lemon zest and thyme leaves then store in the fridge. Deep fry the basil leaves (a quick and easy method is coating in oil and placing in a microwave for one minute).

Lightly sauté the shallots for the pea stock. Add the vegetable stock and bring to the boil, then add the peas and boil for three minutes. Finally blitz in a blender and pass the stock through a fine sieve.

Melt the butter for the risotto in a pan, add the shallots and garlic and sweat until softened. Add the rice and stir for a couple of minutes until the grains are translucent. Gradually add the pea stock, 100ml at a time, until the rice is cooked but remains al dente. Remove the pan from the heat and add the cooked peas and shelled broad beans. Check for seasoning and keep warm.

When ready, heat the olive oil in a non-stick pan and sauté the fillets of red mullet, skin side down, for two-three minutes. Turn the fillets over and remove the pan from the heat.

To serve, arrange the risotto with a mould on the plate and sit the fish gently on top. Place the Mascarpone in a quenelle on top of the red mullet and garnish with the basil leaves and lemon slices.

CHRIS WHEELDON
DOWN HALL COUNTRY HOUSE HOTEL
Hertfordshire, England

Pan fried red mullet tart with salad of tomato and aubergine caviar, baby mozzarella with pesto and balsamico dressing

serves 4

4 x 80-120g fillets of red mullet
200g puff pastry
30g egg yolk
2 packets squid ink
120g butter
1 clove garlic
1 sprig lemon thyme
baby basil leaves for garnish

aubergine caviar
2 aubergines
1 clove garlic, sliced
juice of 1 lemon
20g lemon thyme
100ml olive oil
25g fresh coriander, chopped

4 plum tomatoes
juice of 2 lemons
100g baby mozarella
20g pesto
300ml 10 year old balsamic vinegar
100ml olive oil

First de-bone the red mullet with a sharp filleting knife (or ask your fishmonger to do it for you). Roll out the puff pastry to 5mm thick, place on a non-stick baking sheet, and brush with a mix of the egg yolk and squid ink. Then top with baking paper, cover with a second baking sheet, and bake for 30-40 minutes at 160°C.

For the aubergine caviar, cut the aubergines in half lengthways and score the flesh with a paring knife. Pour a little olive oil into a hot pan and pan fry to golden brown. Place the fried aubergines on a roasting tray, add the garlic and lemon thyme, pour over a little more olive oil, season with salt and milled white pepper and cook in the oven at 180°C for approximately 25 minutes: the flesh should be very soft when you take it out of the oven. Scrape out the flesh with a spoon and, on a chopping board, chop it to a fine purée. Add salt, pepper, lemon juice and chopped coriander, and reserve in a cool place.

Cut a cross in the bottoms of the tomatoes with a paring knife and immerse them in boiling water for 15 seconds, then remove and place in iced water. Remove the skin, and slice and season the flesh with salt, pepper, lemon juice (keep a little for cooking the fish) and olive oil. Mix the baby mozzarella with the pesto and seasoning in a bowl. Place the balsamic vinegar in a stainless steel sauté pan and reduce to a syrup, then add 100ml of olive oil and season with salt and pepper.

When ready, place a few drops of olive oil in a hot frying pan and place the seasoned fish skin side down. Cook until golden and nearly done, then turn and finish with fresh butter, a drop of lemon juice and a little garlic and lemon thyme. Remove the fillets from the pan and keep warm.

To serve cut the baked puff pastry into four rectangles roughly 3 x 8cm. Place one pastry layer in the middle of each plate, cover each first with the tomato slices then aubergine caviar, followed by mozzarella. Top with the red mullet fillets. Finish the plate with small drops of the balsamic reduction and garnish with fresh baby basil leaves.

ARNAUD THULLIEZ : PISCES, SOUK MADINAT JUMEIRAH
MADINAT JUMEIRAH, THE ARABIAN RESORT – DUBAI
Dubai, United Arab Emirates

John Dory 'Demi-Deuil'
with a cappuccino of truffle butter and chablis

GERARD MOUTOU

OASIS BEACH HOTEL

Dubai, United Arab Emirates

Thinly slice the truffle, keeping the ends for the cappuccino. Peel and thinly slice the potatoes with a mandolin. Soak the slices in salted water for an hour, then remove, dry, and brush one side of each slice with egg yolk.

Season each fish fillet with salt and pepper and place four truffles slices evenly on one side of each fillet. Wrap each fillet with the potato slices, egg side in.

Sauté the shallots in a small amount of butter. Add the chablis to the pan and reduce until semi dry, then add the cream and bring to the boil. Reduce again by half and add the butter; do not let the pan boil. Season with salt and pepper and strain the liquid, then add a few truffle trimmings and 2-3 drops of lemon juice and mix well.

Steam the whole leek until cooked and slice diagonally, then sauté the leek slices with clarified butter until browned. Roughly chop and brown the hazelnuts in a dry frying pan, then add the butter, baby spinach, salt and pepper and cook for two minutes. Peel the pearl onions and glaze them in a separate pan until brown with the sugar, water, salt and butter.

To prepare the mousseline Hollandaise, beat the egg yolks with a pinch of fine salt and a little water over a pan of boiling water until the yolks are white. Take off the heat and continue beating gently, then pour in the clarified butter and continue beating to a light yellow emulsion. Side beat the cream (not too thickly): warm both the cream and emulsion and combine the two. Rectify the seasoning with ground white pepper, and serve in a glass topped with the whipped cream (and a little crushed black truffle if desired).

For the blinis, mix the yeast with the warm milk. Add the flours, a pinch of salt, whole eggs, and melted butter and leave covered in a warm place to rest for two hours. After resting, stiffly beat and incorporate first the egg whites, then the whipped cream. Cook the blinis one at a time in clarified butter.

When ready, pan fry the John Dory in clarified butter until slightly browned. Arrange the fillets in a cross on the plate alongside a piece of leek. Divide each of the blinis into three pieces; place two pieces on each plate topped with small amount of baby spinach and a pearl onion. Quarter fill a shot glass for each serving with truffle butter, topped with a spoonful of mousseline Hollandaise and the remaining chopped truffles. Present the cappuccino with a teaspoon on top, and garnish the plate with 2-3 pieces of chervil.

serves 4

8 fillets John Dory, 70-80g each
80g black truffles
3 large potatoes
1 egg yolk

cappuccino
150g shallots, chopped
250ml chablis
150g butter
8g cream
pinch of salt
pinch of white pepper powder
dash of lemon juice

mousseline Hollandaise
2 egg yolks
100g clarified butter
50ml cream
50ml whipped cream

garnish
1 stalk leek
50g hazelnuts
300g baby spinach
30g butter
8 pearl onions
pinch each salt & pepper
pinch of sugar
chervil

blinis
10g live yeast
20ml warm milk
100g white flour
100g rye flour
3 eggs whole
100g butter, melted
2 egg whites
100ml whipped cream
clarified butter
pinch of salt

Salad of smoked eel and smoked trout sausage
on a potato pancake

This dish is reminiscent of the smoked fish-blini combination so much a part of special occasion eating of my Russian childhood. These pancakes, however, are less of a chore to make than traditional blini. The smoked trout sausage is simple and worth mastering as it can stand alone, steamed or lightly grilled. served with salad or a creamy mash. The potato pancakes are a great way to use up leftover mashed potato and are delicious served warm, topped simply with cured or smoked salmon. So if you are making either of these it is worth making a little extra, and the quantities below reflect this.

Before you begin to prepare the smoked trout sausages make sure the fish, egg white and cream are well chilled. Working quickly, blend the salmon to a fine purée in a processor. Add the egg white and continue until it is well combined, then gradually pulse in half the cream. Transfer the mixture to a stainless steel bowl and fold in the smoked trout. Leave the bowl in the fridge for half an hour, then fold in the rest of the chilled cream. Add the chopped chives and season with salt and pepper, then return the bowl to the fridge.

Cut aluminium foil into ten 15cm squares. Place two tablespoons of the sausage mixture on each square, then roll the foil into sausage shapes and twist both ends tightly for a neat finish. Refrigerate for at least an hour, then simmer the sausages gently in water for two minutes. If not using immediately, lay out on a tray to cool then store in the fridge. When ready to serve, remove the sausages from their foil and grill, or coat with butter and cook in the oven.

For the pancakes, warm the mashed potato and beat in the egg until there are no lumps. Fold in sifted flour then whisk in the warm milk and season. Whisk the egg white until stiff, then fold through the potato mix. Press 20g quantities into discs about 7cm in diameter. Pan fry in a little oil, turning the pancakes half way through cooking and ensuring both sides are golden. Store on absorbent kitchen paper when done. Trim with a 7cm cutter, and finish by reheating the pancakes for ten minutes on a baking tray in the oven at 160°C.

When ready to serve, toss the salad leaves in the dressing and layer a square of smoked eel, 3 or 4 diagonal slices of lightly grilled sausage, and a slice of bacon on a warmed potato pancake on each plate. Drizzle the remaining dressing over and around the salad, with a quenelle of horseradish cream on top.

serves 4

4 pieces boned & skinned smoked eel fillet, each about 5cms square

4 very thin bacon slices, fried crisp

a generous handful
seasonal baby salad greens

dressing

6 tablespoons olive oil, mixed with

2 tablespoons red wine vinegar

1 tablespoon freshly grated horseradish combined with 3 tablespoons pure cream

*smoked trout sausage
(makes 10 sausages)*

300g salmon, cleaned,
boned, trimmed & chopped

1 smoked trout,
skinned boned & diced

1 egg white

200ml thick double cream

1 tablespoon chopped chives

*potato pancakes
(makes about 15 pancakes)*

150g dry mashed potato

1 egg

70ml milk, warmed

1 tablespoon self raising flour

1 egg white

ALLA WOLF-TASKER
LAKE HOUSE
Victoria, Australia

Wild sea bass, colcannon, Pommery mustard ice-cream and red wine reduction

serves 4

4 x 150g wild sea bass fillets, de-scaled
4 sprigs chervil
tomato petals

saffron tuile
25cm oblong template
500g butter
250g plain flour
5 egg yolks
5 egg whites
1 pinch saffron threads

colcannon
600g red rooster (or similar) potatoes
6 spring onions, sliced
60ml olive oil

ice cream
25ml milk
360ml semi-whipped cream
20g sugar
9 egg yolks
2 tablespoons Pommery mustard

reduction
400ml red wine
200ml port wine

For the saffron tuile, cream the butter, flour and egg yolk together. Add the saffron to the egg whites and whisk to stiff peaks, then fold into the yolk mix and season to taste. Spread the paste onto a baking sheet using the template and bake in a 180°C oven for 4 minutes, then rest the tuile on a stainless steal ring until it is firm, cool and shaped.

Peel and boil the potatoes, then mash them. Meanwhile gently fry the spring onions until tender. Combine the spring onions and mash, adding olive oil to achieve the required consistency, then season to taste.

For the ice-cream, bring the milk and cream to the boil, whisk the sugar and egg yolks together, then combine and cook out gently until the mixture thickens. Add the mustard and churn in an ice-cream machine.

For the reduction, simply bring the alcohol to the boil in a pan and reduce to a syrup

When ready, pan fry the sea bass fillets skin side down in a non stick pan for 4-5 minutes on a moderate heat until the skin is crispy and the flesh on the inside has nearly cooked through. Turn the fillets over and reserve: the fish will carry on cooking under its own heat. Reheat and arrange the colcannon mash in a ring on the plate, top with a fillet, place the tuile on top and ice cream as shown. Garnish with chervil, tomato petals, and the red wine reduction.

IAIN JURGENSEN
ST ANDREWS BAY GOLF RESORT & SPA
St Andrews, Scotland

Bass on Savoy cabbage in Veltliner

serves 6

6 x 120-140g sea bass fillets
6 strips ham
(San Daniele or Volcano)
6 large potatoes
750 Grüner Veltliner wine
juice of half a lemon

half a Savoy cabbage
3 small onions, finely chopped

mash
500g potatoes
50ml milk
a pinch nutmeg

stewed onions
12 small onions
25g sugar
125ml court-bouillon or chicken bouillon
50ml balsamic vinegar

sauce
80g onions, sliced
50g button mushrooms, sliced
1 sprig thyme
250ml court-bouillon
or chicken bouillon
500ml cream
60g butter, diced & held on ice
Cayenne pepper

olive oil
butter

Slice the large potatoes into long thin strips. Water them well, then wrap the strips as tightly as possible in four sections around a steel rolling pin covered with baking paper to make four hollow cylinders. Coat the rings with oil and bake at 160°C for 10 minutes or so until crisp.

For the stewed onions, caramelise the onions in oil and sugar in an oven proof pan, then add 250ml of the wine and bring to the boil. Add the bouillon, then add salt, pepper, the balsamic vinegar, and a knob of butter and slowly stew in the oven.

Slice and quickly boil the Savoy cabbage in lightly salted water: the green will need slightly longer than the white. Sweat the onions in butter until they lose their colour, then add the Savoy cabbage and stew slowly with plenty of butter, add salt and pepper.

For the mash, peel and halve the potatoes, boil until soft, then drain for a few minutes. Mash then pass through a sieve for a very fine purée, then add 50g soft butter and 30ml cold-pressed olive oil, plus hot milk for a creamy finish. Stir in the nutmeg and keep warm.

Lightly coat the ham in oil and grill until crisp.

For the white wine sauce sweat the mushrooms, thyme and onions, then add the add the remaining 500ml of wine and bring to the boil. Add the court-bouillon and the cream and slowly reduce; leave the sauce quite liquid, then pass through a sieve and blend in the cold butter and Cayenne and check the seasoning.

Carefully fill the crispy potato rings with the mash. Season the bass and cook in a hot pan skin side down in a little olive oil. Add lemon juice, then turn the fillets and cook for a short time on the other side.

FRANZ WÖGERER

THURNHERS ALPENHOF

Zürs an Arlberg, Austria

Plantain wrapped Anegada Mahi Mahi, Caribbean lobster and mango gastrique, coriander oil

ALEX CHEN

CANEEL BAY, A ROSEWOOD RESORT

US Virgin Islands, Caribbean

serves 4

100-150g Mahi Mahi fillet
225g Caribbean lobster meat,
roasted, shelled, & diced
100ml olive oil
4 shallots, shaved
6 cloves garlic, shaved
2 jalapeño, diced & cooked in butter
2 red peppers,
roasted skinned & diced
juice of 4 limes
120g light brown sugar
2 ripe mangoes, diced
50g butter

2 plantains
50g clarified butter

3 sweet potatoes, peeled & cubed
125g butter
125ml cream
1 cinnamon stick, toasted & ground

coriander oil

1 bunch coriander, chopped
5g coriander seeds
50ml olive oil

Peel and slice the plantain lengthways and spread on cling film: allow 4 slices per serving. Brush the slices with clarified butter and season with salt and toasted and ground coriander seeds. Place the Mahi Mahi in the centre and wrap the plantain around the fish, using the plastic wrap to wrap tightly. Twist the ends to remove air pockets and refrigerate to solidify. Remove from the fridge and take off the cling film. Sear seam side down first, then flip them over and finish in the oven for approximately 4 minutes at 180°C until golden brown.

Simmer the sweet potato cubes in salted water. When tender, place through ricer and whip in the softened butter and cream. Season with the cinnamon and salt and pepper, then transfer to a piping bag pending plating.

For the Caribbean lobster and mango gastrique, add the shallots, garlic, and brunoise jalapeños to the olive oil in a sauté pan over a medium-high heat. Add the red peppers and deglaze with the lime juice. Whisk in the sugar until the liquid is a syrup consistency. Just before plating add the lobster, mango, coriander and butter until the sauce has emulsified.

For the coriander oil, blanch and refresh the chopped leaves, drain well, and blend with the toasted coriander seeds and olive oil. Season with salt and pepper and strain through a cheese cloth. Reserve in a squeeze bottle for plating.

To serve, arrange sweet potato purée in the centre of the plate and spoon the lobster-mango gastrique around it. Place the plantain wrapped Mahi Mahi on the purée. Garnish with sweet potato chips, cilantro plush and coriander oil.

Rainbow maki and tempura bento box

serves 4

Rainbow maki
200g tuna
200g snapper
200g (12-16) tiger prawn
100g smoked eel
100g yellow tail (hamachi)
60 pieces flying fish roe
200g cucumber
2 strings of green onions
1 avocado
1 teaspoon sesame seeds
500g sushi rice
2 sheets nori (seaweed)
sweet vinegar for soaking

Boil the prawns in water for one minute, then soak in the sweet vinegar for 30 minutes. Slice the cucumber and avocado.

Spread the sushi rice evenly over the seaweed sheets, sprinkling sesame seeds on top. Flip the sheet over, arrange the avocado and cucumber on top: again sprinkle with sesame seeds. Roll up the sheets. Wrap the prawns, tuna, snapper, and smoked eel around the outside of the roll. Using a sushi mat press the roll to ensure firmness, then cut each roll into 16 pieces, sprinkling each piece with flying fish roe and green onion.

bento box
1.5 litres tempura mix
200g (12-16) tiger prawn
100g aubergine
100g courgette
100g broccoli
125g Japanese rice
4 x 150-200g chicken breasts
1 teaspoon sesame seeds
4 tablespoons Teriyaki sauce

Boil the rice for 30 minutes.

Cut the courgettes, aubergines and broccoli into your preferred size and shape, then coat the vegetables and prawns in the tempura mix. Deep fry each piece in hot oil until golden brown, then drain the cooked pieces on kitchen paper before transferring to a plate.

Season the chicken breast with a little salt and pepper and grill for 18 minutes or so. Set the chicken next to the tempura pieces, brush with teriyaki sauce, and sprinkle with sesame seeds. Serve with the boiled Japanese rice.

TAIKO

THE CRANE

St Philip, Barbados

ABBEY WELL® ~ EVERYWHERE

unlucky for some

ABBEY WELL®

NATURAL MINERAL WATER

We're very precious about ABBEY WELL®. We don't like to see it wasted. It's good, wholesome and comes from a natural resource. Nothing is added except, in some cases, carbon dioxide to make the water sparkle.

While we can't all be lucky we can be careful in our choice of drinks. All too often we are offered sugary soft drinks or alcohol or a mixture of the two. Perfect for some occasions but not all. There is an alternative.

To have enjoyed the pure, clean taste of ABBEY WELL®, which fell at least 3000 years ago, as rain or snow before the age of pollution, you will have experienced the ultimate in pure natural refreshment.

ABBEY WELL® natural mineral water, Still or Sparkling, is available to discerning, consumers everywhere. It's very precious so carry it carefully!

The Essence of Quality

Mosaic of foie gras, apple jelly, fig and prune chutney

makes 10 servings

prune purée

100g prunes soaked in Armanac for 2 weeks
50ml stock syrup

chutney

60g prunes soaked in Armanac
20g diced shallot
6 fresh figs
25ml sherry vinegar
half a teaspoon whole grain mustard
half a clove garlic
25g sultanas
2 teaspoons sugar
2 teaspoons chopped tarragon
a pinch salt
a pinch Cayenne pepper

apple jelly

10 red apples
juice of half a lemon
1 teaspoon sugar
1.5 leaves gelatine

terrine

1 lobe foie gras, about 500g
50ml Armagnac
20 semi-dried grapes
12 shiitake mushrooms
25g butter
half a clove garlic
1 sprig thyme
2 outer green leaves Savoy cabbage

fig crisp

4 fresh figs
half a teaspoon liquid glucose
half a teaspoon caster sugar

GRAEME SHAW
NORTON HOUSE
Edinburgh, Scotland

A lot of the preparation can be done well in advance. Drying the red grapes – cooking in a low oven until half their original size – takes a couple of hours and can be done the day before, by which time you will have already been soaking your prunes in Armagnac for thirteen days. You'll also need to prepare for the apple jelly the day before by removing the cores and chopping the apples, then heating the chopped apple in a pan with the sugar and lemon juice and stewing until the apple breaks down. Transfer the contents to a muslin and leave to drip overnight to yield about 300ml of apple juice. Finally, blend all the ingredients for the fig crisps until smooth, spread the paste thinly on a silpat mat to your desired shapes, and cook in a low oven at 70°C until dry: this too will take a couple of hours and can be done at the same time as the grapes.

Bring the foie gras to room temperature so it is pliable, then lay it out on cling film and with a sharp knife remove all the main veins, then remould back into its original shape. Place the lobe in a shallow tray and marinade with 50ml of Armagnac for 20 minutes, then season with salt and pepper and heat in a low oven until the foie gras reaches 37°C.

Meanwhile removed the stems from the mushrooms and sauté with the butter, garlic and thyme until soft, then drain on kitchen towels to remove any excess fat. Trim the cabbage leaves into squares, removing the main veins. Blanch the leaves in salted water until tender, then refresh in cold water.

To assemble the terrine allow the foie gras to cool slightly then split it into three equal pieces. Line a square terrine mould, approximately 120mm x 120mm, with cling film. Place the first piece of foie gras into the clingfilm lined mould, followed by a layer of mushrooms and dried grapes and topped with cabbage. Repeat this process once more and finish with the remaining foie gras, then press and refrigerate. Slice the terrine straight from the fridge and allow to stand for 10-15 minutes to reach room temperature, then brush with olive oil and lightly sprinkle with Maldon salt.

For the fig and prune chutney bring all the ingredients to the boil in a heavy saucepan, then lower the heat and simmer for 2 hours, adding a little water if the mixture becomes too dry before the 2 hours is completed. Leave to cool, then liquidise to the consistency of jam.

Purée the Armagnac-soaked prunes with the stock syrup until a smooth sauce consistency is achieved. Warm the apple juice for the jelly, then dissolve the gelatine leaves in the liquid and leave to cool and set.

Serve as shown.

Coriander, garlic and chili spiced chicken salad with mango salsa

250g chicken tender fillets
2 teaspoons olive oil

marinade
2 tablespoons fresh coriander, chopped
1 medium red bell pepper, seeded
1 hot chilli pepper, seeded
2 cloves garlic, roughly chopped
1 small fresh ginger root, scraped & roughly chopped
2 teaspoons sweet chilli sauce
2 teaspoons honey
2 teaspoons vegetable oil
2 teaspoons paprika powder
salt and pepper to taste

mixed garden salad
200g mixed garden leaves
6 fresh asparagus spears, cooked & cut into strips
1 red bell pepper, roasted & cut into strips
1 yellow pepper, roasted & cut into strips
50g fine French green beans, freshly cooked
8 cherry tomatoes, halved
1 medium carrot, cut into julienne strips & blanched
50g sugar snap peas, cut into julienne strips & blanched

mango salsa
1 firm ripe mango, finely diced
2 teaspoons coriander, finely chopped
1 teaspoon lime juice
1 teaspoon olive oil

serves 2

Blend the marinade ingredients together. Season the chicken strips with salt and pepper and place in the marinade for 30 minutes. Heat the oil in a heavy sauté pan. Place the chicken in the hot oil, one piece at a time, and lightly brown on both sides. Remove from the sauté pan, place on a baking tray and finish in the oven at 180°C for approximately 4 minutes.

Combine the salsa ingredients and season with salt and pepper. Toss all the salad ingredients in a bowl with olive oil, salt and pepper.

Arrange the salad in the centre of large plates. Place the cooked chicken tenders on top with mango salsa over and around the salad.

GRAHAM LICORISH
CORAL REEF CLUB
St James, Barbados, West Indies

Roast poussin, étuvée of pak choi and puy lentils, truffle sauce

DAVID MCCANN
DROMOLAND CASTLE
County Clare, Republic of Ireland

serves 4

poussin

4 x 350g poussin
4 small cloves garlic
4 sage leaves
4 small shallots
knob of butter
8 rashers streaky bacon

duxelle

100ml cream
2 diced shallots
12 button mushrooms, chopped
6 girolles

étuvee

250g pak choi
50g Puy lentils
50g carrot
50g celeriac
50g peas
1 small red onion
20g duck fat (or butter)

4 x 15g slices foie gras

mash

2 good mashing potatoes
200ml cream
20g butter
pinch of nutmeg

sauce

300ml chicken and veal demi-glace
100ml Madeira
10g black truffle
15g unsalted butter

Remove and leave the poussin legs to one side. Extract the wishbone and fill the cavity of each bird with a garlic clove, a sage leaf and a sliced shallot; season with salt and milled pepper. Cut the legs in two at the joint. Trim the bones on each end of the drum stick and de-bone and trim the thighs.

To prepare the duxelle sweat the sliced shallots in a little butter, then add the girolles and button mushrooms and cook until dry. Moisten with a little cream, season well, and leave to cool.

Place pairs of thighs together on two rashers of bacon with duxelle inside each thigh. Roll and tightly wrap each pair together in cling film and poach in water at 80°C for 15 minutes. Roast the poussin crowns at 170°C for 15 minutes, turning and basting regularly. Remove the crowns from the roasting tray and cook the drumsticks in the oil and juices until well done.

Soak the lentils in cold water for 1 hour, then cook in simmering salted water for 15 minutes. Wash and slice the pak choi: peel and dice the vegetables. Sweat the greens and vegetables in the fat or butter: the onion first, then the celeriac and carrot, and when tender add the peas. Toss in the leaves at the last minute and cook quickly, checking the seasoning.

Peel and cut the potatoes into small pieces and cook in boiling salted water until tender. Drain well and pass through a medium sieve. Boil the butter and cream together, season with nutmeg, and mix well into the puréed potato.

For the sauce, finely chop and sweat the truffle. Add the Madeira and reduce by half, then add the demi glace and reduce again by half. Finally stir in the butter off the heat and check the seasoning.

When ready, in a hot pan quickly sauté and season the foie gras slices. Remove the breast from the bone, colour the thighs in a little butter and carve. Assemble the dish as shown in the photograph.

Poussin breast and confit leg
with shallot tart and foie gras velouté

Remove and set aside the poussin legs. Poach the body in simmering chicken stock for 5 minutes, then remove and stand on its wishbone end to cool, reserving the stock: the chicken should still be a little raw in the middle. Remove the breasts from the crown and check for gristle or bone.

Confit the legs by immersing in olive oil on a low temperature (100-110°C) for two and a half hours. Remove, allow to cool, and trim ready for finishing.

For the foie gras velouté, reduce 400ml of the chicken stock by half with the garlic, thyme, and bay leaf. Add approximately 50g of the foie gras trimmings and allow to soften. Using a stem blender, blend the foie gras into the stock: at this stage it should still be runny, but thick enough to coat the back of a spoon. Pass this off and whisk in 30g of butter and 50ml of cream: after seasoning this is now ready.

To make the tart, cook the shallots in a little butter with a few thyme leaves and seasoning, then spread over the puff pastry in a round baking tin and bake at 190°C for 25 minutes until golden brown.

Heat a little olive oil in a small pan, and add the onions and seasoning. When the onions have a little colour add 20g of butter, a sprig of thyme and bay. Continue to cook the onions gently in the foaming butter until soft, then pour off excess butter and add 20ml of chicken stock. Lightly reduce to glaze. Cook the salsify by the same method.

Gently fry the bacon lardons until golden, but not crispy and dry. Gently wilt the watercress with a little butter and season well.

To finish the dish, heat a little oil in a non-stick pan and place the poussin breasts skin side down: season. Add the confit leg and continue to fry until golden, then add 15g of butter. Allow the butter to foam slightly whilst basting the poussin. Finally, add 60ml of chicken stock and pull the meat to the side to simmer till cooked. The dish is now ready for assembly as shown.

serves 2

1 x 500g poussin
1 litre chicken stock

foie gras velouté
75g foie gras trimmings
half a clove garlic, chopped
1 sprig thyme, chopped
half a bay leaf
50ml double cream

tart
2 banana shallots, finely sliced
1 x 10cm puff pastry disc

garnish
3 baby onions
3 bâtons salsify
2 sprigs thyme, chopped
2 bay leaves
15g smoked bacon cut into lardons
10g watercress

olive oil
butter

JOHN CAMPBELL
THE VINEYARD AT STOCKCROSS
Berkshire, England

Tropical Lady poulet

ORLANDO SATCHELL
LADERA RESORT
Soufrière, St Lucia

serves 4

4 chicken breasts
2 egg whites
200ml cream
2 small onion, chopped
4 spring onions, chopped
2 small red chilli peppers, chopped
2 clove garlic

2 ripe plantains, diced & fried
60ml olive oil
120ml Tropical Lady liqueur
500ml demi-glace

Place 2 chicken breasts, cream, and egg whites in the food processor. Add half the onion, spring onions, peppers, garlic, and salt and pepper. Blend together, adding the plantain when the mixture is a smooth mousse.

Season the other chicken breast, form a pocket and fill it with mousse.

Put the olive oil in a hot sauce pan: add the remaining half of the ingredients and sauté for two minutes, then add the liqueur and demi-glace. Bring to the boil and reduce, adding salt and pepper to taste.

Pan-sear the chicken breast until both sides are golden brown: finish cooking in oven for 10-15 minutes at 180°C. Serve as shown.

New Forest duckling with aubergine and honey sauce.

Preparation time: 120 minutes
Cooking time: 120 minutes

serves 4

4 whole ducklings
700g duck fat
(enough to cover the trimmed legs)
12g coarse salt

1 clove garlic
4 sprigs thyme
4 tablespoon honey

sauce
2 aubergines
4 cloves garlic
4 sprigs thyme
500ml tomato fondue
1 onion, sliced
250g honey
100ml virgin olive oil
25ml sherry vinegar

2 waxy potatoes
50g butter
1 sprig thyme

4 slices foie gras
selection of seasonal vegetable

savoury caramel
200ml duck stock
2 tablespoons sherry vinegar
400g caster sugar
ground white pepper

Remove the legs from the ducklings. Trim and remove the excess fat, rub the legs with coarse salt and leave for four hours, then brush off any remaining salt and dry the legs with kitchen towel. Place the legs in a deep baking dish, cover with the duck fat, and bake in the oven at 80°C for 2 hours.

Trim the excess fat and sinew from the duck breast. Vacuum pack each breast with a slice of garlic, a sprig of thyme and a teaspoon of honey. Slow cook the breasts in simmering water for 45 minutes at 50-55°C, then remove and chill.

For the honey sauce, slice the aubergines into 1cm thick slices and char grill on both sides. Place the aubergine on a baking tray and cover with garlic, thyme, tomato fondue, sliced onion, honey, salt and pepper. Bake in the oven until cooked through for 20 minutes at 200°C. Remove and cool. Blend half the cooked aubergine with the oil and sherry vinegar to make the sauce. Reserve the remaining aubergines for the final dish.

Cut the potatoes into 4cm high cylinders. Place in a heavy bottom sauce pan, cover with water and add the butter, thyme, and salt and pepper. Cook over a medium-high heat until all the liquor has reduced.

Panfry the sliced foie gras until browned on both sides. Steam the vegetables for 3 minutes, then brush with orange scented clarified butter (the zest of half an orange in 50g of clarified butter) and finish with salt and pepper.

For the caramel tree, bring the duck stock, sherry vinegar and ground white pepper to the boil in a copper pan, then add the sugar. Continue to boil, and reduce to a caramel reaching 160°C. Transfer the caramel to a piping bag with which to form shapes.

MARTIN MATYSIK
THATCHED COTTAGE HOTEL & RESTAURANT
Hampshire, England

Roast breast of duck, green beans and fresh almonds, seared foie gras, argan oil and white peach

AIDAN MCGRATH

SHEEN FALLS LODGE

County Kerry, Republic of Ireland

Season and seal the duck breasts in a hot pan with the oil, turning frequently until cooked. Remove from the pan and rest on a wire rack.

Halve the peaches; keep one of the halves to segment for garnish and dice the other three.

To make the sauce, sauté the shallots and diced peaches, add the sugar and cook until caramelised. Add the liqueur, flambé, and reduce until only a little of the liquid is left. Add the jus, bring to the boil and reduce until the sauce coats the back of a spoon.

To heat the beans boil a little water, butter, and seasoning in a small pan. Add the beans and almonds and toss until hot, then pour off the water, add a little more butter and argan oil to glaze the vegetables, and season.

Dip the peach segments for garnish in sugar and glaze in a hot non stick pan. Season, sear, and rest the foie gras. Warm the duck if required before slicing.

When ready to serve, arrange the beans and almonds on the plate. Position slices of duck on top of the beans with foie gras on top and peaches around; drizzle the plate with the sauce and a little argan oil.

serves 4

4 breasts of duck, skinned
4 x 100g slices foie gras
2 white peaches

sauce
4 shallots, sliced
25g Muscovado sugar
25ml peach brandy
(or other peach liqueur)
500ml duck or veal jus

200g French beans,
blanched, topped but not tailed
200g broad beans,
blanched & shelled
200g runner beans,
sliced & blanched
150g fresh almonds, shelled
argan oil to season
sea salt and milled white pepper
olive oil
butter

Grenadin of local veal with wild mushroom and Madeira jus, celeriac and potato dauphinoise and baby vegetables

serves 4

4 x 200g veal fillet
2 tablespoons veal fat or oil

jus
1 glass Madeira
600ml veal stock
1 shallot, finely chopped
25g butter

250g wild mushrooms
50g butter
half a bunch parsley, chopped

dauphinoise
2 large onions, sliced
50g unsalted butter
600ml double cream
2 cloves garlic, crushed
200g celeriac, thinly sliced
450g potatoes, thinly sliced

Heat the oven to 180°C. Cook the onions for the dauphinoise in half the butter for 2-3 minutes without colouring, then allow to cool. Bring the cream to the boil with the garlic and remaining butter and season with salt and pepper. Arrange the onion, potatoes and celeriac into layers in an oven proof dish, making sure the potatoes are the top and bottom layers: overlap the top layer of potato slices to give a neater finish. Pour over the cream, making sure the potatoes are covered, and bake for 45-60 minutes until the vegetables are tender and have absorbed all the cream. Keep warm to one side until ready to serve.

For the jus, reduce the Madeira with the shallots, add the veal stock, bring the pan to the boil and reduce to half. Monté with the butter and season, then put to one side and keep warm.

Sauté the wild mushrooms in the butter and parsley and keep warm. Coat the veal in the fat or oil and grill for 5 minutes on each side, but ensuring the meat is still pink in the middle. Put to one side and keep warm.

Set the dauphinoise on the plate with sliced veal fillet on top, then wild mushrooms. Arrange baby vegetables around the plate, add Madeira sauce, and serve.

DIDIER BIENAIME
ROSEVINE HOTEL
Cornwall, England

Triple dish of veal
with Périgord truffles and American artichoke stew

RAINER SIGG
HOTEL BALTSCHUG KEMPINSKI MOSCOW
Moscow, Russian Federation

With a small sharp knife delicately separate the bones from the veal tail, passing the knife along the bones again and again. Trim off the fat and gristle and keep them for the sauce. Lay out the trimmed veal tail on foil, score with a sharp knife and spread with a thin layer of minced veal. Put the lentils on top and delicately roll up the tail. Cover the roll with the raw pork caul and tie securely with string.

Finely chop the bones and trimmings and fry in hot fat in a heavy based pan, then add the diced garlic and vegetables for a couple of minutes until browned. Add the tomato paste, pour in the wine and stock and bring to the boil.

Season the outside of the tail roll and brown all over in a little oil in a separate pan. Transfer the tail to the sauce pan and stew uncovered for 1.5-2 hours in the oven at 180°C. Take the tail from the sauce; when cold, remove the string and cut into 2cm slices. Slice the foie gras to 7mm slices of the same diameter: place foie gras slices on the tail slices and roll each serving in caul.

Filter the cooking sauce through muslin and boil until reduced to 200ml. Finely dice the truffles, warm in a little butter, pour over the alcohol and boil until dry, then add the reduced cooking sauce. Stir in the cold butter to finish.

Scar the veal loin, add the vegetables, herbs, and veal stock, and cook for about an hour on the hob, then take out and cut the loin into 1cm cubes. Take 200g of the cooking stock, reduce by half, add the sour cream, and warm the veal cubes in the liquid, adding the whipped cream to finish.

Put the potatoes into salted cold water, cook, and mash. Mix the nutmeg, salt and pepper with the sour cream and melted butter and mix over and into the mash.

Cut the artichoke into boat shapes with a slightly hollowed hull. Warm up in butter, pour over the chicken stock and stew to the desired degree of hardness.

Sear the seasoned veal cutlets in a little butter, then transfer to the oven at 180°C and cook to a golden yellow. Cut the truffles into equal cubes and mix with the butter and breadcrumbs. Fry the cutlets in seasoned butter, then spread with the truffle and breadcrumb mix.

When ready, slightly fry veal tail rolls, foie gras side down, then turn over and cook to readiness in the oven for another 2-3 minutes at 180°C.

serves 4

veal tail

1 veal tail
30g minced veal
60g lentils
stewed in seasoned grape vinegar
20g pork caul
1 clove garlic, chopped
1 shalott, chopped
half a carrot, finely diced
half a stalk celery, finely diced
half a teaspoon tomato paste
375ml red wine
1 litre veal stock
60g foie gras

truffle sauce

broth from veal tail
10g Périgord truffles
10g butter for truffles
50ml each cognac & Madeira
10g cold butter to finish

blanket (stewed veal)

200g veal loin
half a carrot, diced
1 celery stalk, diced
1 shalott, diced
cuttings of parsley & bay leaf
1 litre veal stock
100g sour cream
1 dessert spoon whipped cream

mashed potatoes

100g potatoes
150g sour cream
10g butter
nutmeg

artichoke

4 equal pieces American artichoke
10 g of butter
500ml chicken stock

veal fillet

4 x 80g veal cutlets
20g Périgord truffles
15g butter
15g bread crumb
a sprig each thyme and rosemary
butter

Slow cooked belly of pork, whole grain mustard crust, potato purée and broad beans

serves 4

1kg pork belly
4 teaspoons wholegrain mustard
200g potato
40g broad beans
40g fresh peas

sauce
4 shallots, diced
4 Cox apples, diced
8 sage leaves
100ml brandy
200ml veal jus
150g butter

caramel apple
4 crab apples
400ml stock syrup
400ml caramel

garnish
4 sage leaves

butter
olive oil

Slow cook the pork for 90 minutes in a 100°C oven, then rest for ten minute. Remove and deep fry the skin until crispy. Coat the pork with mustard and grill slightly, then keep warm until needed.

Sauté the shallots, sage and apple, add the brandy and veal jus and reduce by half. Pass though a sieve, then slowly whisk in the butter, correct the seasoning and keep warm.

Remove the core from the crab apples and blanch in the stock syrup for 5 minutes, then drain and coat in the melted caramel. Transfer the coated apples to a tray lined with baking paper and leave them to set.

Peel and dice the potatoes, cook in boiling water for 5 minutes, then drain and purée though a sieve with 60g of butter. Season and keep warm. Pod the peas and cook in boiling water for 5 minutes, then transfer to a blender and purée. Add butter and seasoning to taste, pass though a sieve and keep warm. Remove the broad beans from their pods and blanch in boiling salted water for 3 minutes, then strain, sauté in olive oil and season.

Brush each sage leaf for the garnish in oil and microwave for 1 minute on a flat plate.

Trim the pork into portions. Pipe potato purée onto the plate with pork on top. Pour pea purée onto plate and assemble broad beans around. Arrange the apple, crisped sage and crackling on the plate and pour sauce around.

STEPHEN SWEETING

CAREYS MANOR HOTEL

Hampshire, England

Slow braised pork belly wrapped in Parma ham, fricassée of white beans, squid, garlic, parsley, lemon confit, creamed lobster sauce

LUKE TIPPING

SIMPSON'S RESTAURANT

Birmingham, England

Preparation must begin a day in advance. Use a sharp knife to cut the skin off the pork. Remove the bones and even out the thickness, taking a slice from the thicker areas and replacing it where the meat is thinner. Firmly roll up and tie the belly into an even-shaped roll.

Heat the olive oil, vanilla, star anise, cardamom, coriander, peppercorns and bay leaf in a shallow cast iron casserole with a lid and carefully place the pork in the oil. Bring back to the boil, cover the pan, and transfer to the oven at 120ºC for 3-4 hours until the meat feels very tender.

Lift out the meat and set it aside to rest on a plate. Carefully remove the string and lay out the meat on a long strip of cling film. Spread Parma ham along the pork and roll into a sausage shape. Seal the cling film around the roll, then seal again in foil twisting the ends to ensure a tight parcel. Place in the fridge overnight.

For the sauce, chop up the lobster head with a heavy knife. Heat some olive oil in a saucepan and sauté the lobster shells for 3 minutes, then add the peppers, tomatoes and shallot and cook for 5 minutes until soft. Cover with water, bring to the boil, lower the heat and simmer for 30 minutes.

Strain the liquor through a sieve into another pan, pressing the shells with the back of a small ladle to extract as much flavour as possible. Bring the liquor back to the boil, stir in the cream and bring to a simmer, then cook gently for 4 -5 minutes. Check the seasoning and keep warm.

For the fricassée, clean and slice the squid into circles. Place the parsley, lemon, garlic and oil in food processor, whiz together, then set aside.

To serve, remove the pork from the fridge and with a sharp carving knife slice into portions about 1cm wide, then remove the foil and cling film. Season and flour the pork, dusting off any excess, then pan-fry in hot oil for 2 minutes on each side.

Meanwhile fry the squid quickly in olive oil, to seal but not to colour, season with salt, then add the white beans, parsley, garlic and lemon mixture. Arrange the fricassée in a bowl with the pork on top. Using a whisk or hand blender, whip up the lobster sauce to create a foam, spoon the bubbles around the plate, and serve.

serves 4

1 pork belly
1 litre olive oil
1 vanilla pod, split
3 star anise
1 teaspoon cardamom pods
1 teaspoon coriander seed
1 teaspoon pink pepper corns
1 bay leaf
2 packets sliced Parma ham

1 lobster head
5 tomatoes, chopped
1 red pepper, chopped
1 shallot, chopped
100ml double cream

100g baby squid
25g flat parsley
1 clove garlic
1 teaspoon lemon zest
100ml olive oil
150g cooked white beans

Pecan crusted lamb ribeye, wild mountain greens, sweet potato charlotte, port wine and fig demi glace

serves 4

2 800g lamb racks
1 jar Dijon mustard

pecan crust
100g pecan nuts
8 slices fresh white bread, crust removed
1 bunch parsley leaves, stems removed
4 sprigs thyme, stems removed
half a cup chopped chives
100ml extra virgin olive oil

charlotte
1.5 sweet potatoes, peeled & diced
4 orange segments
4 lemon segments
1 cinnamon stick
2 star anise
4 sprigs mint

100g double cream
100g butter

mountain greens
225g assorted baby greens (kale, mustard greens, turnip greens etc) washed & cut into thin strips
4 cloves garlic, sliced
zest of 1 orange

demi-glace
100ml port wine
4 sprigs thyme
1 shallot, sliced
110g dried figs, halved & softened in hot water
225ml demi glace
60g unsalted butter

Place all the ingredients for the pecan crust in a food processor. With the machine running, drizzle the olive oil in a steady stream.

Remove the bones and trim any excess fat and sinew from the racks of lamb, then shape the racks to resemble a miniature prime rib by leaving a tail piece. Cut each rack in half to yield 4 miniature roasts. Season the racks with salt and pepper and sear over a high heat until golden brown and delicious. Remove from the pan and coat each piece with a generous amount of Dijon mustard. Coat each roast with the pecan crust and cook to your desired extent in a preheated 180°C oven about 20 minutes for medium. Allow the lamb to rest for 10-15 minutes before serving to allow the meat to retain its juices when sliced.

The potatoes should be prepared in advance and reheated. Make a simple syrup by bringing all the ingredients except the potatoes and mint to the boil in a litre of water. When this mixture is boiling add the potatoes and mint: reduce the heat and cook slowly until the potatoes are fork tender. Remove the pan from the heat and allow the potatoes to cool completely in the syrup: overnight is best. When cool, remove and pass the potatoes through a ricer. When ready, reheat the purée with the cream and butter and season with salt and pepper.

Reduce the port wine with the thyme and shallot until almost dry. Add the demi glace and reduce again to the desired consistency. Whisk in the butter and seasoning. Halve the figs and heat in hot water unter softened. Drain and stir the the figs into the demi-glace using a little of the hot fig water if the consistency needs adjusting.

The mountain greens must be prepared at the last minute and served immediately. Heat the olive oil in a skillet and add the garlic. When the garlic begins to brown add the zest and greens and cook over a high heat until the greens are slightly crispy. Season with salt and pepper and serve.

JOSEPH TRUEX
CHATEAU ELAN
Georgia, USA

Stuffed saddle of lamb

serves 4

1kg saddle of lamb
400g caul fat
16 slices streaky bacon
16 confit tomatoes
75g Parmesan shavings
40g pistou (pesto)

stuffed cabbage leaves
4 large Savoy cabbage leaves
150g cooked cepes,
bordelaise style
200g cooked foie gras
300g chicken force meat

sauce
7 juniper berries
500ml orange juice
150g honey
700ml lamb stock
2 lemon grass stalks

To prepare the sauce, dry roast the juniper berries then deglaze the pan with the orange juice and honey. Add the stock and lemongrass and reduce to the required consistency. Pass through a sieve, season, and keep warm.

Bone the saddle, and remove all the fat and sinew, keeping the fillet intact. Lay the saddle out flat and spread a layer each of confit tomatoes, pesto and Parmesan over the middle. Season, then roll the fillet over and wrap and tie a layer each first of bacon rashers, then caul fat. Seal on all sides, then roast for 9 minutes at 200°C. Leave to rest before slicing for serving.

For the stuffed cabbage, blanch the cabbage leaves and cut a disc with a large pastry cutter. Combine the sautéd cepes, chopped foie gras and force meat. Place each leaf in turn on a sheet of cling film with a quarter of the filling mix. Make a neat ball and securely wrap the cling film around. Steam the balls for 6 minutes and serve.

MARTIN ROBERTS
DOMAINE COCAGNE
Cagnes-Sur-Mer, France

Fillet of Lamb with char-grilled Provençal vegetables, garlic rösti and a rosemary jus

serves 2

2 lamb fillets

rösti
1 baking potato
1 clove garlic, crushed
1 red onion

vegetables
1 aubergine
1 medium tomato
1 courgette
1 red onion
20g French beans
2 thin slices pancetta
1 bunch chopped parley
1 bunch of rosemary
olive oil

jus
1kg lamb bone
1 leek
1 onion
1 carrot
2 cloves garlic
1 bay leaf
5 peppercorns
1 bouquet garni

Marinade the lamb fillets in good quality olive oil and a few sprigs of rosemary.

To prepare the jus, chop and roast the lamb bone in the oven until brown. Cover with water, add the remaining ingredients, bring to the boil and simmer for 6 hours, then strain and reserve. Transfer the stock to a separate pan, add two sprigs of rosemary, and reduce until the sauce begins to thicken. This can be prepared 24 hours in advance.

For the garlic rösti, place the baking potato in a pot of water and bring to the boil. Take the pan off the heat and leave the potato to cool in the water. When cool, peel off the skin, then grate with a large size grater and mix with the garlic, one diced red onion and the chopped parsley. Press into two small patties approximately 1 cm thick and leave to set. These too can be prepared up to 24 hours in advance and left covered in the fridge.

Halve the aubergine, tomato and courgette, brush with oil and char-grill (cut side down first) on a skillet pan. Top and tail the beans, blanch in boiling water, separate into two bunches, and wrap a slice of pancetta around each bunch.

Place the grilled vegetables on a baking tray, drizzle lightly with olive oil, and place in the oven at 150ºC. After 5 minutes seal the lamb fillet in a hot pan. Place the lamb in the oven with the French beans for a further 5 minutes. Meanwhile, fry the röstis on both sides in the pan used to seal the lamb. Rest the lamb on a cooling rack for one minute while layering the vegetables and rösti on warmed plates; top with the sliced lamb and drizzle the plate with warmed rosemary jus.

CHRIS TURNER
THE PRIORY BAY HOTEL
Isle of Wight, England

Cannon of salt marsh Welsh lamb, fondant potato, leek and courgette spaghetti, shiraz, mint and rosemary reduction

serves 4

1 long saddle
salt marsh Welsh lamb
18 rashers rindless pancetta
6 small potatoes
300ml stock
1 large leek
2 courgettes

reduction
150ml demi-glace
375ml shiraz red wine
a sprig each mint & rosemary
225g butter

Remove the two eyes of the lamb from the saddle. Cut each eye into three and wrap each portion in pancetta.

Peel and cut the potatoes into round shapes with a cutter. Stand the cylinders in an oven proof dish half covered in stock and with a knob of butter on each for glazing, sprinkle with salt and pepper, and cook in the oven at 170°C for about 30 minutes until soft in the centre.

Cut the leek and courgette lengthways thinly, cook quickly with a small amount of water, drain, toss in a knob of butter to make them shine, add salt and pepper to taste, and spin the vegetables on a fork to create a ball.

Reduce the demi-glace, red wine, mint and rosemary leaves (leave a little for garnish) in a pan until it coats the back of the spoon, then pass through a fine strainer.

Pan sear the cannons of lamb for approximately 5 minutes. Slice each cannon into three; the meat should be pink in the centre. Arrange as shown, garnished with the remainder of the mint and rosemary. Enjoy.

PHILIP MARTIN
GREEN BOUGH HOTEL
Cheshire, England

Terrine of quail with herb and black pepper jelly, carrot and poppyseed dressing

serves 4

2 quail
4 slices Parma ham
30g trompette mushrooms, chopped

mousse
2 chicken breasts, chilled
2 egg whites
200ml cream

jelly
10 leaves gelatine
400ml chicken stock
1 bunch parsley
1 bunch tarragon
2 tablespoons cracked black pepper
1 head broccoli, cooked

dressing:
50g carrot, diced
1 clove garlic, diced
1 shallot, diced
100ml olive oil
caraway seeds
6 tablespoons white wine
poppy seeds

Prepare the chicken mousse by blending the chilled chicken breasts to a paste. Press the paste through a sieve, then add the egg whites and cream and bind together. Store the mousse in the fridge until needed.

With a sharp knife take off the quail breasts, season, and sear in a hot pan, them allow them to cool. Take off and bone the quail legs, stuff the cavity with chicken mousse, and wrap each leg tightly in cling film. Poach the wrapped legs for 10 minutes in the chicken stock.

To prepare the terrine, line the dish with cling film, leaving enough overhang to cover the top, and cover the sides and base with a 1cm thick layer of chicken mousse. Cover the mousse with a layer of Parma ham. Next, mix the remaining chicken mousse, quail breasts and trompette mushrooms together, seasoned with salt and pepper. Fill the Terrine dish with the mixture until the top is level. Fold over the cling film, cover the dish with tin foil, and cook in a bain-marie at 160°C for about an hour, or until it reaches an internal temperature of 74°C. Remove the dish and leave to cool.

To make the jelly, soak the gelatine in cold water and bring the chicken stock to the boil. Take the pan off the heat and add the gelatine, cracked black pepper, herbs, and the small florets from the top of the broccoli.

Spread out a layer of cling film. When the jelly mix is almost set, pour it out onto the cling film and allow it to go cold, then cut out six rectangles slightly larger than the corresponding faces of the terrine. Remove the terrine from the fridge, take off the cling film, and glaze the faces with some reserved gelatine. Roll the terrine in the jelly until all sides are covered, trimming off any excess. Wrap in cling film and return the terrine to the fridge until required.

For the dressing, sauté the carrot, garlic and shallot in the olive oil until cooked, then add the caraway seeds and 100ml of water. Cook for 3 minutes, then purée, place back in the pot and return to the boil. Allow the liquid to go cold then add the vinegar, olive oil and seasoning. Finish with poppy seeds.

When ready, warm the stuffed quail legs in the oven. Carefully slice and place the terrine alongside the sliced quail leg; drizzle carrot and poppy dressing on the plate (if it is too thick, add a little more oil), add fresh salad leaves, and serve.

ROBERT WEBSTER
BALLYNAHINCH CASTLE HOTEL
Galway, Republic of Ireland

Roasted quail
with tortellini of wild mushrooms, porcini and truffle sauce

DALE GARTLAND AND NEIL BRAZIER
THE LODGE AT KAURI CLIFFS
Kerikeri, New Zealand

To prepare the pasta, sieve the dry ingredients into a food processor and whisk the remaining ingredients together. While the processor is running add the liquids: stop the machine when the mixture is just past a breadcrumb texture. Form the dough into a ball and wrap in cling film, then rest in the fridge for at least 2 hours.

For the mousse, dice the chicken breast then blend it with a pinch of salt in a food processor for 1 minute. Add 40g of the cream, then press through a fine sieve into a bowl over ice and blend in the remaining cream. Trim and cook the mushrooms (keep the trimmings for the sauce), shallots, garlic and tarragon in a pan with 10g of butter. Allow the mushrooms to cool, then roughly chop and fold the mushrooms and seasoning into the mousse. Wrap a small amount in cling film and poach in boiling water for 3 minutes to test the consistency – add more cream if too firm – and seasoning.

Roll out the dough on a pasta machine at its thinnest setting and cut out circles with a 9cm cutter. Place one and a half tablespoons of mousse in the centre of the disc and shape the tortellini.

Sweat the shallots, garlic and thyme for the sauce in 30g of butter with a pinch of salt for 5 minutes (no colour), then add the porcini powder and mushroom trimmings and cook for a further 2 minutes. Add the wine and reduce by half, then the chicken stock and reduce by half again. Finally add the cream, bring to the boil, and simmer for 10 minutes. Pour through a fine sieve and whisk in the remaining butter. Adjust the seasoning and use a hand blender to achieve a foam effect. Keep warm.

When ready, place the quail in a pan with a knob of butter and a teaspoon of oil and cook for 2 minutes on each side and then 2 minutes on the backbone. Take out and rest. Cook the tortellini in salted water for 4 minutes. Carve the breasts and legs off the quail, reheating if necessary. Place garnish on plate, then meat, adding the sauce at the last moment.

serves 4

4 quail

pasta
125g plain flour
2 egg yolks
1 whole egg
10g truffle oil
pinch of salt

mousse
100g chicken breast
105g double cream
100g mixed oyster and shiitake mushrooms
40g shallots, chopped
1 clove garlic, crushed
5g chopped tarragon
butter

sauce
60g shallot, sliced
1 clove garlic
1 sprig thyme
5g porcini powder
90g mushroom trimmings
200ml white wine
200ml chicken stock
150ml cream
70g butter
truffle oil to taste

garnish
broad beans
celeriac batons
roast parsnip
chervil
enoki and trompette mushrooms

Ostrich fillet parcels

serves 6 as a starter

6 sheets filo pastry
2 tablespoons melted unsalted butter

filling

250g ostrich fillet cut into thin strips
1 onion, finely chopped
50g pine nuts
2 cloves garlic, crushed
1 teaspoon ground cumin
1 teaspoon ground cardamom
a pinch cayenne pepper
2 pinches ground cinnamon
2 teaspoons ground turmeric
100g mushrooms, chopped
60ml Makweti red pepper & tomato chutney
1 tablespoon apricot jam
black pepper
chives
olive oil

chutney

1 large onion
1 red pepper
3 chopped tomatoes
100g sugar
200ml vinegar
20ml oil
pinch of salt

First prepare a batch of Makweti red pepper and tomato chutney. Cut the onion and pepper into thin slices and cook in the oil until soft but not brown. Add the rest of the ingredients and leave to simmer until it thickens, then allow to cool.

Coat each filo sheet with melted butter. Press the sheets to double thickness into the 6 hollows of a muffin pan to await the filling.

Heat a tablespoon of olive oil in a frying pan. Cook the onion over a medium-low heat until soft but not browned (5-6 minutes), then add the pine nuts, garlic, cumin, cardamom, cayenne, cinnamon, and turmeric and cook for another 2-3 minutes. Add the mushrooms and cook until soft, finally adding the chutney and apricot jam. Check the seasoning and transfer the mix to a bowl.

Heat another tablespoon of olive oil in the frying pan and stir-fry the steak until it changes colour. Return the mushroom mixture to the pan and combine. Adjust the seasoning if required.

Spoon the filling into the filo-lined hollows. Cut around the hollows and close each parcel with a light twist. Bake at 180°C until lightly coloured (about 10 minutes).

To serve, tie a chive around the neck of each parcel and accompany with fresh tomatoes and mango chutney.

FREDELEESHA BYL

MAKWETI SAFARI LODGE
Limpopo Province, South Africa

Medallions of rabbit saddle and black pudding wrapped in bacon, wholegrain mustard sauce

MARK DONOHUE

ADARE MANOR HOTEL & GOLF RESORT

County Limerick, Republic of Ireland

serves 4

350-400g rabbit saddle
50g black pudding, crumbled
2 slices back bacon
2 shallots, finely chopped
2 scallions, finely chopped
1 sprig chopped thyme
20ml chicken stock
1 teaspoon butter

chutney
100g chopped prunes
2 pears, peeled and chopped
50ml cider
25ml white wine
25ml white wine vinegar
25g white sugar
25g brown sugar
1 teaspoon mixed spice

brioche
250g strong flour
12g sugar
pinch of salt
3 eggs
150g unsalted butter
40ml tepid milk
10g fresh yeast

mustard cream
25g shallots, chopped
25g butter
50ml white wine
50ml chicken stock
100ml cream
1 teaspoon wholegrain mustard

Remove the bone from the rabbit leaving the belly flaps intact. Lay the bacon out flat on a work top, then place the rabbit on top. Sweat the shallots and thyme in the butter, then mix in the black pudding, scallions and a little of the chicken stock to form a smooth paste.

Fill the cavity of the rabbit with the black pudding mix, then roll the saddle into a cylinder covered by bacon, wrap tightly in cling film, and chill.

Mix all the ingredients for the chutney in a heavy based pot and simmer for approximately 1 hour until dry, then leave to cool.

For the brioche, sieve the dry ingredients into a bowl. Add the warm milk and yeast and mix to a smooth dough, gradually adding the softened butter. Leave to prove until the dough has doubled in size, then knock back and place in a greased loaf tin. Prove for a further 20-25 minutes, then bake at 190°C for 15-20 minutes until the top is brown and risen. Leave the bread to cool.

To prepare the mustard cream, sweat the shallots in the melted butter, then add the white wine and reduce by half. Add chicken stock and reduce again by half, finally add the cream, bring to the boil, and simmer for 10 minutes. Pass through a fine sieve, stir in the mustard, and season.

When ready, slice the rabbit into 8 pieces and pan fry on both sides until golden brown (about 2 minutes per side). Warm the sauce; slice and toast the brioche. Serve with the chutney as shown.

Fillet of Kintyre sika venison
with Parisienne potatoes and a red wine reduction

serves 4

1 venison fillet
1.5 kilo large potatoes.
500ml good game stock
750ml good red wine
butter and olive oil

Here in Kintyre we have a spectacular range of natural produce available from the sea and the hills. There are red, roe and sika deer literally on our doorstep: for flavour and tenderness the sika is the finest of all.

First peel the potatoes and with a large Parisienne spoon (a special spoon-shaped cutter) scoop out potato balls. Pat these dry and cook in a frying pan with lots of butter and seasoning until they are golden brown and tender; this can also be done in the oven, and will take ten to fifteen minutes.

Meanwhile trim off any sinew, cut the venison fillet into medallions, and season with salt and black pepper. Heat a small amount of olive oil in a heavy bottomed sauté pan and sear the medallions on both sides until nice and brown and the juices are sealed in. Place in a hot oven (200°C) for three minutes then turn over and cook for a further three minutes. Remove from the oven and keep warm.

For the red wine reduction add the red wine and stock to the sauté pan and boil vigorously to a syrupy consistency; be very careful not to over-reduce the sauce or it will taste bitter.

To serve, arrange your choice of vegetables on a warm plate and place the venison on top. Arrange the Parisienne potatoes around the outside and serve with a sauce boat of red wine reduction.

ANGUS MACDIARMID
BALINAKILL COUNTRY HOUSE
Argyll, Scotland

Springbok fillet carpaccio

ROBERTO DE CARVALHO

THE TWELVE APOSTLES HOTEL & SPA

Cape Town, South Africa

To prepare the pesto, purée all the ingredients in a food processor until smooth. Season with salt and pepper. The pesto can be made 3 days ahead and chilled covered with cling film.

Trim the springbok fillet. Mix the herbs and black pepper on a plate, roll the fillet in them, then roll up the fillet in cling film so that it resembles a sausage. Place in the freezer for at least 30 minutes to become half-frozen and easier to slice later.

Place the quartered tomatoes on a baking sheet, sprinkle with the Maldon sea salt and cook in the oven at 95°C for about 2 hours until they resemble soft sundried tomatoes. Remove the tomatoes from the oven, discard any excess salt and allow to cool.

Unwrap the springbok fillet and, using a sharp knife or a slicing machine, slice into wafer thin medallions. Arrange the medallions around 4 plates. Toss the rocket leaves in about 25ml of the pesto and place a handful of leaves in the centre of the plate. Place the slow roasted tomatoes and Pecorino shavings on the salad, however you feel looks good, with some shoots for garnish. Drizzle each plate with the grapeseed oil, and serve immediately.

This lovely starter or light meal can be enjoyed all year round. Springbok meat is very low in fat; likewise, the use of grapeseed oil is very healthy (and incorporates yet another part of the Cape in the dish). The peppery flavour and deep green colour of the rocket leaves create a simple but fantastic salad, the Pecorino cheese adds pungency: together, carpaccio, rocket, Pecorino, grapeseed oil and slow roasted tomatoes are simply magnificent.

serves 4

250g springbok fillet
30g fresh thyme, chopped
30g fresh rosemary, chopped
1 fresh bay leaf, chopped
20g freshly cracked black pepper
500g plum tomatoes, quartered
60g Pecorino cheese,
shaved with a vegetable peeler
35ml grapeseed oil
80g rocket leaves, washed
25g Maldon sea salt

fresh coriander pesto
(makes about 500ml)

2 cups packed fresh coriander
leaves, washed well
2 cups packed fresh Italian parsley
leaves, washed well
half a cup pine nuts, toasted until
golden, cooled, & finely chopped
half a cup freshly grated Parmesan
3 large cloves garlic, minced
half a cup Paarl grapeseed oil

ABBEY WELL® IN CRYSTAL

quality through clarity

ABBEY WELL®

NATURAL MINERAL WATER

Many regard it as a simple glass of water. To many
others it's a pure art form.

To hold a beautully balanced, finely crafted, crystal leaded
goblet is itself a delight. To fill it with ABBEY WELL®
natural mineral water is to bring together the best of both
worlds – quality through clarity.

To have enjoyed the pure, clean taste of ABBEY WELL®,
which fell at least 3000 years ago, as rain or snow before
the age of pollution, you will have experienced the
ultimate in natural refreshment.

ABBEY WELL® natural mineral water, Still or Sparkling, is
available to discerning, consumers everywhere.

The Essence of Quality

Assiette of strawberry and champagne

serves 4

*vanilla crema cotta
and strawberry compote*
600 ml whipping cream
70g sugar
quarter of a vanilla pod
2 leaves gelatine

10 strawberries cut into 4
50ml strawberry coulis

strawberry and port sorbet
50g sugar
1 teaspoon glucose
300ml strawberry coulis
(bought or liquidised fresh berries)
50ml port

pink champagne jelly
10g caster sugar
250ml champagne
half a leaf gelatine

sablé paste
100g unsalted butter
50g sugar
1 small egg yolk
1 coffee spoon of cream
125g flour
half a vanilla pod

strawberry sablé
100ml whipping cream
10g sugar
a splash of brandy
10 strawberries, quartered

Vanilla crema cotta and strawberry compote
Bring the cream, sugar and vanilla to the boil. Soak the gelatine leaves in cold water then dissolve into the mix and pass through a fine sieve. Cool over ice until just setting, then transfer the custard to moulds and chill for at least six hours. For the compote, slightly warm the strawberries in the coulis, then chill.

Strawberry and port sorbet
Bring the sugar and glucose to the boil in 50ml water to make 100ml of stock syrup. Pour the warm syrup over the coulis and port, then churn in an ice cream machine until frozen and smooth. If you don't have an ice cream machine, stand the bowl on iced salt in the freezer and stir frequently until set.

Pink champagne jelly
Warm the sugar in a splash of champagne, then dissolve the soaked gelatine in the liquid. Pour the mix into the rest of the champagne, stir gently, and set in shot glasses. NB: the less you stir, the fresher and bubblier it will be.

Strawberry sablé
Beat the sugar and butter for the paste until light and fluffy, then add the yolk and cream and quickly beat in the flour. Chill for 30 minutes, then roll out to 5mm and cut into 12 discs. Chill for a further 20 minutes, then bake at 150°C for about 25 minutes until slightly coloured.

Whip the cream, sugar and brandy until firm then pipe onto one of the discs of biscuit and arrange strawberries around the rim. Repeat, and top with the last biscuit.

Arrange all the components on the plate and garnish with mint, strawberries, and icing sugar.

JAMES PEYTON
AMBERLEY CASTLE
West Sussex, England

Peach Melba on almond biscuit

Place all the sugared nuts ingredients in a large, heavy-based non-stick frying pan and, over the lowest possible heat, gently melt the sugar. Stir occasionally, being very careful once the sugar starts to caramelise; the aim is individual white, sugarcoated nuts. Transfer the nuts to a very lightly oiled tray and allow to cool. These can be kept for a few days in an airtight container.

Blitz all the ingredients for the raspberry purée in a liquidiser. Pass the mixture through a fine sieve into a bowl and set aside.

For the almond biscuits, combine the flour, Amaretti biscuits, sugar and salt in a large bowl. Cut the butter into chunks and, with your fingertips, rub it into the flour mixture until well incorporated. Mix the egg yolk and milk together, then add to the bowl, binding the mixture together with the fingertips until the pastry comes together. Divide into 2 equal balls, wrap in cling film and chill for at least 1 hour. When ready to use the pastry, remove it from the fridge and work it with your hands until it becomes soft and elastic. Then, on a lightly floured surface, roll the pastry out as thinly as you dare. Using a round, 5cm cutter, cut out the biscuits and place them on a baking sheet covered with greaseproof paper. Bake the biscuits for about 10 minutes at 180°C until lightly golden. Remove from the oven and place on a wire rack to cool. The biscuits will keep for several days in an airtight container.

For the ice cream, combine the cream and milk in a saucepan, place on a moderate heat and bring to just about boiling point. Add the mint, stir thoroughly, and remove from the heat. Leave to infuse for at least an hour: any less and you won't get that great depth of mint flavour. Gently reheat the mint-infused milk and cream mixture and remove the mint. In a large bowl, whisk the egg yolks and sugar together. Still whisking, carefully add the hot, mint-infused milk and cream. Return the mixture to the pan and, over a low heat, stir continuously until the custard coats the back of a wooden spoon. Remove from the heat immediately and strain through a fine sieve into a jug. Leave to cool completely before churning to a soft consistency in an ice cream maker. Freeze in a suitable container.

Halve the peaches and place them in a pan of sugar syrup. Heat the syrup very gently, poaching the peaches until the skins slip off easily (about 1-2 minutes).

To assemble the Melba fill the centre of each peach with mint ice cream. Place an almond biscuit in the centre of each serving plate, then sit a peach on top. Scatter sugared nuts around the biscuits and, just before serving, drizzle over raspberry purée.

serves 6

Everything except the poached peaches can be prepared well in advance

6 ripe, juicy peaches
350ml sugar syrup

sugared nuts
25g pine kernels
25g whole peeled almonds
25g whole peeled hazelnuts
25g chopped pecan nuts
110g icing sugar
4 tablespoons Grand Marnier

raspberry purée
225g raspberries
juice of 1 lime
3 tablespoon icing sugar
55ml framboise (raspberry liqueur), optional

almond shortbread biscuits (makes about 30 biscuits)
225g soft plain flour, sifted, plus extra for rolling
50g Amaretti biscuits, finely ground in a food processor
75g golden caster sugar
a good pinch of salt
175g unsalted butter, softened
1 egg yolk
2 tablespoons milk

garden mint ice cream
10 portions
600ml double cream
300ml full fat milk
a large bunch of fresh mint
9 egg yolks
200g caster sugar

Apple and vanilla parfait with mincemeat parcels

serves 8

apple sorbet
300ml apple juice
125ml cider
2 tablespoons glucose
3 Bramley apples,
peeled & sliced
juice of 1 lemon

parfait
4 eggs, separated
170g caster sugar
1 vanilla pod, split
460ml double cream

parcel filling
100g currents
100g sultanas
75g brown sugar
1 cinnamon stick
pinch of Nutmeg and mixed spice
100g suet
130ml brandy
200ml Guinness
zest of 1 lemon or 1 orange
1 apple, grated

parcel pastry
1 packet of filo pastry
150g melted butter

The apple and vanilla parfait needs to be prepared a day in advance.

Slowly cook all the sorbet ingredients together until the apple slices are tender, then blitz and pass through a sieve. Allow the mix to cool, then churn in an ice cream maker and store in the freezer.

Whisk the egg yolks until pale and fluffy; in a separate bowl whisk the egg whites to a peak. Boil the sugar in a little water, and when it reaches 120°C pour half over the whites and half over the yolks. Continue whisking both until they are cool.

Whip the cream and vanilla together to a soft peak. Gently fold the cream into the yolks, then fold the whites into the mix. Fill moulds half way up with the vanilla parfait mix, add a scoop of apple sorbet, then fill to the top with more parfait. Freeze for 24 hours.

To prepare the parcel filling, place all the mincemeat ingredients except the suet in a pan and leave them to steep for an hour. Move the pan to a low heat and cook for 2 hours, then add the suet and cook for a further 30 minutes. Take the pan off the heat and leave it to cool.

For the parcel, lay one sheet of filo pastry flat, brush it with melted butter, then place another sheet on top. Cut the double thickness into eight strips, and brush the edges of each with melted butter; Place a tablespoon of mincemeat at the end of each strip and roll: the result should be the size of a spring roll. Brush all over with melted butter and cook until nicely browned (about 10 minutes) at 190°C.

Serve as shown.

CHARLIE LAKIN
FEVERSHAM ARMS HOTEL
Yorkshire, England

Banana-Rama

Banana toffee pie, banana and vanilla crème brulée,
baby banana tarte Tatin with rum and raisin ice cream

makes 12 portions

raspberry coulis for serving

crème brulée
450ml double cream
150ml banana purée
125g sugar
8 egg yolks
1 vanilla pod
Sugar for glazing

tarte Tatin
12 baby bananas
12 small squares puff pastry
60g sugar
a small amount of water
icing sugar for glazing

banana toffee pie
200ml condensed milk
3 bananas
100ml double cream
12 raspberries
25g grated chocolate
12 cooked small sweet pastry cases
Icing sugar for glazing
100ml whipped cream

For the crème brûlée, split the vanilla pod lengthways into four. Bring the purée (150g of banana, liquidised), cream and vanilla pod to the boil. Whisk the sugar and egg yolks together and add to the boiling cream mixture. Pass through a sieve to remove the vanilla pod and pour the mix into cups or ramekins and cook in a bain marie at 110°C for 45 minutes or until just firm. Cool, sprinkle with the sugar and glaze under the grill or with a blow torch.

Peel the baby bananas. Slowly cook the water and sugar on a low heat to a light caramel: this will take about ten minutes. Wrap the puff pastry around the baby bananas, leaving part of the banana exposed. Pour the caramel onto a non stick baking tray and stick the exposed side of the banana into the caramel. Bake at 180°C for about 15 minutes or until golden brown.

Simmer the condensed milk in a pan for approximately 4 hours or until it turns into toffee. Thinly slice the bananas and layer them on the bottom of each pastry case, then pour the toffee over the top. Place another layer of sliced banana on top, dust with icing sugar, and caramelise with a blowtorch or under the grill. Pipe a small amount of whipped cream on top, add a raspberry, and sprinkle with the grated chocolate.

CHRIS WHEELER
STOKE PARK CLUB
Buckinghamshire, England

ice cream

75g raisins

15ml dark rum

1 litre double cream

60g glucose

14 egg yolks

350g sugar

12 small brandy snap baskets

Soak the raisins in the rum. Boil the cream with the glucose. Whisk the yolks and sugar together and slowly pour into the cream mix, whisking well. Return the pan to the heat and simmer, stirring until it thickens, but don't let it boil. Strain and leave to cool, then churn for about 8 minutes in an ice cream maker. Add the soaked raisins and churn again for two minutes or until the ice cream is ready.

To serve, pipe a zig zag on each plate using raspberry coulis (or chocolate or toffee sauce). Place a crème brûlée at one end of each plate, with a tarte Tatin next to it. Place a brandy snap basket next to the tarte Tatin with a scoop of ice cream inside the basket. Place the Banana toffee pie next to the ice cream. Sprinkle the plate with icing sugar and garnish with caramel.

Rhubarb meringue tart

1kg rhubarb cut into 3cm lengths
3 egg yolks
120g Demerara sugar
2 tablespoons plain flour
3 egg whites
pinch salt
3 tablespoons caster sugar
sweet pastry

Line a 26cm pastry case – preferably with a detachable base – with sweet pastry and bake blind.

Spread rhubarb over the base. Mix together the egg yolks, sugar and flour and spread this over the fruit (or technically the veg). Bake in the oven at 200°C for ten minutes to start the rhubarb cooking.

Meanwhile whisk the egg whites until they are stiff. As they stiffen, trickle in the caster sugar. Take the tart from the oven and spread the meringue on top. Reduce the heat to 180°C and bake for a further 25 minutes.

A few pointers. Use winter 'forced' rhubarb, not the coarse and bitter outdoor variety that reaches the shelves in spring and summer. Forced rhubarb is toothpaste pink and comparatively fragile in flavour. Traditionally grown in Yorkshire, the enterprising Dutch also now offer a thicker, though not superior, winter rhubarb.

The egg whites must be completely free of imperfections – including the yolk – if they are to be successfully whisked. The bowl used must also be dry and clean. Don't add the sugar too early: the whites should already be forming peaks before you start to do so.

SHAUN HILL
THE MONTAGU ARMS HOTEL
Hampshire, England

Pandan pudding with blueberry compote

serves 4

40g fresh pandan leaves
(available in Thai & Malaysian
shops), chopped
200ml skimmed milk
200ml double cream
zest of 1 orange
zest of 1 lemon
1 vanilla pod
6 eggs, separated
100g caster sugar
2 gelatine leaves

blueberry compote
350g blueberries
50g caster sugar
quarter of a cinnamon stick
quarter of a fresh red chilli

Liquidise the pandan leaves and milk until they become a rich green colour. Put the mixture into a pan with the cream and the orange and lemon zest. Split the vanilla pod open and scrape out the seeds, then add the pod and seeds to the pan and bring to the boil. Meanwhile, mix together the egg yolks and half the sugar in a bowl. Pour the pandan mixture onto the yolks, stirring all the time, then return to the pan and cook, stirring constantly, until the mixture has thickened enough to coat the back of the spoon. Remove from the heat. Soak the gelatine leaves in cold water for 5 minutes, then drain well and stir into the custard until dissolved. Pass the mixture through a fine sieve and cool rapidly.

Whisk the egg whites to soft peaks and fold in the remaining sugar. Fold the egg whites into the custard when it is nearly cold, then spoon the mixture into 4 square lined moulds and leave in the fridge to set.

Meanwhile, make the blueberry compote. Heat 250g of the blueberries in a pan with the sugar and a dash of water until the sugar has dissolved, then blitz to a purée in a blender. Add the cinnamon, chilli and remaining blueberries and leave to cool.

To serve, turn out the puddings on to 4 plates. Hollow out a square hole about 5mm deep in each one. Arrange the blueberries from the compote in lines in the holes, then pour in enough of the liquid so that the blueberries are almost covered. Serve with the remaining compote.

NEVILLE CAMPBELL

BLAKES HOTEL

London, England

Yummy liquorice pannacotta
with frozen berries and a sabayon swirl

serves 4

500ml double cream
80g caster sugar
6g liquid liquorice (grated)
2 leaves gelatine
250g frozen mixed berries (only about half the bag will be used)

sabayon
2 egg yolks
1 splash sherry or Madeira
50g caster sugar

To make the pannacotta (set chilled custard), heat the double cream and caster sugar in a non-stick saucepan over a medium heat until just coming up to the boil. Add the liquid liquorice and whisk well until it has all melted in.

Place the gelatine leaves in a small bowl, cover with water, and leave for 10 minutes to soak. Remove the leaves and squeeze out any excess water. Add the soaked gelatine leaves to the pan and whisk well in, then pass through a fine sieve into a measuring jug.

Place four pyramid (or dariole) moulds on a small tray or baking sheet. Divide the mixture between the moulds then place in the fridge to set for at least one hour.

To serve, remove the moulds from the fridge and run a sharp knife around the top of each mould. Turn each pannacotta out into the centre of a cold plate. Arrange a small helping of the frozen berries around the outside of each pannacotta.

Finally make the sabayon, which must be done at the last minute but is very quick. Bring 500ml of water to the boil in a deep saucepan and insert a glass pyrex bowl to create a bain-marie. Into the glass bowl place the egg yolks, sugar and a mean splash of the sherry or Madeira. Whisk vigorously until the mixture thickens and comes together and falls off the whisk in ribbons. Spoon a swirl of the sabayon over the frozen berries and eat immediately.

JOHN BENSON-SMITH
HAZLEWOOD CASTLE
Yorkshire, England

Individual cheesecakes with raspberry coulis

serves 8

biscuit base
2 cups graham crackers
or digestive biscuits, crushed
120g melted butter

cheesecake
225g cream cheese, softened
4 egg yolks
100g sugar
2 vanilla pods, cut in half
lengthways & seeds scraped out
12.5g cornflour
175ml double cream
4 egg whites, lightly beaten
1 teaspoon lemon zest

raspberry coulis
300g frozen raspberries in syrup
2 tablespoons sugar
1 teaspoon fresh lemon juice,
or to taste

garnish
225g fresh raspberries

Lightly grease 8 pastry rings or muffin tins with butter. Mix together the crushed biscuits and melted better and press into the bottom of the pastry rings.

Mix the egg yolk with the sugar and vanilla pods until smooth. Add the cornflour, lemon zest and cream cheese and mix again until smooth. Add the cream, then gently add the egg white. Fill the pastry rings (or tins) and cook for about 7 to 8 minutes at 150°C, then remove from the oven and chill.

To make the raspberry coulis, purée the raspberries with their syrup and the sugar and lemon juice in a blender or food processor. Pour the mixture through a fine sieve into a bowl, pressing down on the solids.

Carefully remove the cheesecakes from the pastry rings and serve with the raspberry coulis and fresh raspberries.

EMMANUEL MOTTE
CARL GUSTAF HOTEL
Saint Barthélemy, French West Indies

White chocolate truffle with raspberries encased in a thin chocolate shell topped with blood orange ripple ice cream

For the blood orange syrup, combine the glucose and sugar in a pan with 50ml of water to dissolve the sugar. Boil until the liquid starts to turn golden, then add the juice, being careful to avoid the liquid spitting. Continue boiling until it has reduced by half, then leave to cool and refrigerate.

For the ice cream whisk the egg yolks and sugar in a bowl, then add the liquid glucose and milk powder. In a pan boil the double cream, milk and orange zest, then pour this onto the egg yolk mix and stir until well mixed. Return the mix to the pan and stir over a low heat until the liquid thickens so it lightly coats the back of a wooden spoon: it is very important that you do not allow the liquid to boil. Take the pan off the heat to cool, strain the liquid into a cold container, then refrigerate.

When both the ice cream and blood orange syrup mix are cold, churn the ice cream mix in an ice cream machine, adding half the blood orange syrup at the last minute (keep the other half to decorate the plate) and mixing in slightly so that orange swirls can be seen. Freeze.

Temper the chocolate by heating 90g in the microwave to 40-45°C, stirring regularly. Remove from the microwave and add the rest of the chocolate drops. Stir until the temperature reduces to 27°C, then reheat slightly to 31-32°C. Line moulds with the chocolate. Make a garnish with the leftovers by spreading chocolate on the table and scraping into curls with a 7cm scraper.

Slowly bring all the coulis ingredients to the boil in a pan. Transfer to a blender, liquidise, and pass through a sieve to remove the seeds.

For the white chocolate truffle filling, place the cream in a bowl, add the lime zest and juice and whip until soft peak. Melt and gently fold the chocolate into the cream: it is important not to over-mix. Fold in the raspberries, then fill the chocolate-lined moulds and refrigerate.

Turn out the moulds when ready to serve: these must be well chilled (at least 4 hours). Garnish the plate with blood orange segments, raspberries, coulis, chocolate curls, and the syrup.

serves 4

chocolate shell and curls
110g dark chocolate
use small chocolate couverture drops

ice cream
6 egg yolks
75g sugar
25g liquid glucose
25g milk powder
250ml double cream
250ml milk
zest of one orange

blood orange syrup
25g liquid glucose
50g sugar
300ml blood orange juice

raspberry coulis
100g raspberries
15g sugar
40g liquid glucose
juice of half an orange

white chocolate filling
120g white chocolate
300ml cream
zest of half a lime & a squeeze of the juice
55g fresh raspberries

garnish
blood orange segments
fresh raspberries

KEVIN DOWLING AND SUSAN ROUND
ARMATHWAITE HALL HOTEL
Cumbria, England

Gingerbread and chocolate pudding, St Lucian vanilla ice cream and sun blushed pineapples and chilli

serves 4

gingerbread

250g soft butter
200g brown sugar
400ml dark treacle
6 eggs
900g pastry flour
2 teaspoons baking powder
4 tablespoons dried ginger powder
3 teaspoons ground cinnamon
1 teaspoon ground nutmeg
250ml milk
125ml plain yoghurt
100ml orange juice

chocolate custard

6 egg yolks
75g cornstarch
225g sugar
900ml milk
100g butter
300ml thick cream
250g melted dark chocolate

200g bitter dark chocolate

brandy snaps

1 teaspoon brandy
50g butter
50g sugar
2 tablespoon treacle
50g flour
pinch of salt
half a teaspoon ground ginger
half a teaspoon lemon juice

Gingerbread

Grease and line a deep cake tin with parchment paper. Cream the sugar and butter in a bowl – a kitchen maid is ideal, otherwise use an electric whisk. Whip until light and fluffy, then add first the treacle, then the eggs one by one.

Sieve the flour, baking powder and spices together to mix well. Mix the milk, yoghurt and orange juice together. Beat first the flour mix then the milk mix into the butter and sugar: finish with a good handful of the flour mix. Pour into the tray and bake in pre-warmed oven at 160°C for 50 minutes or until a needle comes out clean.

Chocolate custard

Beat the eggs, cornstarch and sugar together very well. Bring the milk to the boil and beat a little into the egg mix, again mixing very well. Mix all the egg mixture into the milk then return to the heat and bring to a slow boil, stirring constantly. Allow to cook for about 1 minute, then take off the heat and beat in the butter, cream and chocolate until well mixed.

Crush the gingerbread and mix with some of the custard to form a texture similar to a bread stuffing mix. Start with about half the custard then work your way from there. Butter small individual pudding moulds, then roll the inside with sugar and chill well. When cold, roll a piece of the mix into a ball and stuff well into the mould so it is about three quarters full. Drop in a square of chocolate, then roll another smaller ball to fit the top, pressing down well. Now chill until needed. Heat in the oven at 190°C for 10-12 minutes, by when the pudding should fall out of the mould in one piece. If not, leave in the mould.

Brandy snaps

Melt the brandy, butter, sugar and treacle until combined. Allow to cool, then sift in the flour, salt and ginger and mix well, adding the lemon juice as you go, then leave to cool completely in the fridge. Once cooled, roll out and cut into strips and bake one at a time on

JON BENTHAM
ANSE CHASTANET RESORT
St Lucia, Caribbean

parchment paper in the oven at 160°C for 7-8 minutes, by when they should be golden brown all over. When each piece is cool enough to handle cut it to the desired shape: you'll need to work fast as it will go very brittle; return it to the oven to soften again if it does. Store the set pieces in an airtight container. The rest of the snap mix can be frozen or left in the fridge for 8 days.

Pineapple and chilli syrup
Bring the sugar to the boil in 500ml of water then take off the heat and add the remaining ingredients. Allow to cool, then refrigerate until needed.

St Lucian vanilla ice cream
Bring the milk, vanilla pods and seeds, and cream to a slow boil. Beat the egg yolks and sugar together: mix about a third of the hot milk into the egg, beating well, then return the egg mix to the milk and mix in well. Bring this mixture to a slow simmer – do not allow to boil – stirring until it coats the spoon. Take the pan off the heat and chill quickly. When thoroughly cold, churn as per machine settings for ice cream maker. Should the mixture curdle through overcooking, just put into a blender, mix till smooth, then churn.

pineapple and chilli syrup
1 pineapple, peeled & diced
4 black peppercorns, crushed
1 small red chilli,
deseeded & finely chopped
4 cardamon seeds, crushed
6 coriander seeds, crushed
1 strip lemon peel
1 strip orange peel
110g sugar

St Lucian vanilla ice cream
6 egg yolks
200g sugar
450ml milk
450ml thick cream
2 vanilla pods split open
& seeds scraped out: keep seeds

Chocolate duo

serves 6

To make the brownie, first melt the chocolate and the butter over a bain-marie on medium heat in a non-stick saucepan until they are perfectly blended.

Beat the eggs with the yellow sugar in a bowl, then pour in the chocolate mix, stirring continually, until the mixture comes harmoniously together. Set aside.

Place the flour and the yeast in bowl, pour in the chocolate mixture and whisk vigorously.

Transfer the mixture to a buttered and floured mould and cook in the oven at 150ºC for 15 minutes. Remove from the heat and set aside to cool, then cut into squares.

For the pudding, heat the cream with the vanilla string over a bain-marie on medium heat in a non-stick saucepan. Add the chocolate and milk, stirring constantly, until it has all melted in.

Meanwhile, beat the egg yolks with the fine sugar in a bowl. Add the chocolate mixture, stirring at all times. When blended spoon the mixture into six buttered moulds, which have been greased previously with butter. Cook in a bain-marie in the oven for 45 minutes at 140ºC, then leave to cool.

To serve, lay a brownie square on a layer of crème Anglaise. Turn out the puddings, and place on top of the brownie.

brownie
2 eggs
120g good black chocolate
100g butter
100g yellow sugar
120g flour
half a teaspoon yeast

chocolate pudding
170ml cream
half a vanilla string bean
150g good dark chocolate
80ml milk
2 egg yolks
60g fine sugar

JOÃO FERNANDES
QUINTA DA BELA VISTA
Madeira, Portugal

ABBEY WELL® - NATURALLY

the perfect complement

ABBEY WELL®

NATURAL MINERAL WATER

The best natural ingredients plus a combination of knowledge, patience, creativity and energy are the pre-requisites to preparing interesting quality food.

To smell it, to eat it, to enjoy is bliss. To help your palate appreciate the most subtle of flavours there can be no better way to complement the finest of foods than with a glass of ABBEY WELL® natural mineral water.

To have enjoyed the pure, clean taste of ABBEY WELL®, which fell at least 3000 years ago, as rain or snow before the age of pollution, you will have experienced the ultimate in natural refreshment.

ABBEY WELL® natural mineral water, Still or Sparkling, is available to discerning, consumers everywhere.

The Essence of Quality

AFRICA: **South Africa**   ASIA: **Sri Lanka**   AUSTRALASIA: **Australia • New Zealand**
CARIBBEAN: **Anguilla • Barbados • Dominica • St Barthélemy**

Makweti Safari Lodge
Welgevonden Game Reserve
PO Box 310
Vaalwater 0530
Limpopo Province
South Africa
T: +27 11 837 6776
F: +27 11 837 4771
E: makweti@global.co.za

recipe page 116

CuisinArt Resort & Spa
PO Box 2000
Rendezvous Bay
Anguilla
British West Indies
T: +1 264 498 2000
F: +1 264 498 2010
E: reservations@cuisinart.ai

recipe page 58

The Twelve Apostles Hotel & Spa
PO Box 32117, Victoria Road
Camps Bay, 8040
Cape Town
South Africa
T: +27 21 437 9000
F: +27 21 437 9055
E: bookta@rchmail.com

recipe page 122

Coral Reef Club
St James
Barbados
West Indies
T: +1 246 422 2372
F: +1 246 422 1776
E: coral@caribsurf.com

recipe page 84

Lighthouse Hotel & Spa
Dadella
Galle
Sri Lanka
T: +94 91222 4017
F: +94 91222 4021
E: lighthouse@lighthouse.lk

recipe page 30

The Crane
St Philip
Barbados
West Indies
T: +1 246 423 6220
F: +1 246 423 5343
E: info@thecrane.com

recipe page 78

Lake House
King Street
Daylesford
Victoria 3460
Australia
T: +61 (0)3 5348 3329
F: +61 (0)3 5348 3995
E: info@lakehouse.com.au

recipe page 70

Fort Young Hotel
PO Box 519
Victoria Street
Roseau
Dominica
T: +1 767 448 5000
F: +1 767 448 5006
E: fortyoung@cwdom.dm

recipe page 28

The Lodge at Kauri Cliffs
Matauri Bay Road
Northland, PO Box 800
Kerikeri
New Zealand
T: +64 9 407 0010
F: +64 9 407 0061
E: info@kauricliffs.com

recipe page 114

Carl Gustaf Hotel
Rue des Normands
BP 700 - Gustavia
97099 Saint Barthélemy Cedex
French West Indies
T: +59 0590 29 7900
F: +59 0590 27 8237
E: info@hotelcarlgustaf.com

recipe page 140

recipe page 76

Caneel Bay
A Rosewood Resort

PO Box 720
St John
US Virgin Islands
T: +1 340 776 6111
F: +1 340 693 8280
E: caneel
    @rosewoodhotels.com

recipe page 24

Dusit Dubai

133 Sheikh Zayed Road
PO Box 23335
Dubai
United Arab Emirates
T: +971 4 343 3333
F: +971 4 343 4222
E: info@dusitdubai.com

recipe page 144

Anse Chastanet Resort

One Anse Chastanet Road
Soufrière
St Lucia
West Indies
T: +1 758 459 7000
F: +1 758 459 7700
E: ansechastanet@candw.lc

recipe page 20

Jebel Ali
Golf Resort & Spa

PO Box 9255
Dubai
United Arab Emirates
T: +971 4 883 6000
F: +971 4 883 5543
E: jagrs@jaihotels.com

recipe page 62

The Bodyholiday LeSport

PO Box 437
Castries
St Lucia
West Indies
T: +1 758 457 7800
F: +1 758 457 7898
E: lesport@
    thebodyholiday.com

recipes pages 27, 38, 66

Madinat Jumeirah
The Arabian Resort – Dubai

PO Box 75157
Dubai
United Arab Emirates
T: +971 4 366 8888
F: +971 4 366 7788
E: mjinfo@jumeirah.com

recipe page 90

Ladera Resort

PO Box 225
Soufrière
St Lucia
T: +1 758 459 7323
F: +1 758 459 5156
E: ladera@candw.lc

recipe page 32

Le Royal Meridien
Beach Resort & Spa

PO Box 24970
Dubai
United Arab Emirates
T: +971 4 399 5555
F: +971 4 399 5999
E: business@
    leroyalmeridien.com

recipe page 50

Al Maha Desert Resort

PO Box 7631
Dubai
United Arab Emirates
T: +971 4 303 4222
F: +971 4 343 9696
E: almaha@emirates.com

recipe page 68

Oasis Beach Hotel

PO Box 26500
Dubai
United Arab Emirates
T: +971 4 399 4444
F: +971 4 399 4200
E: obh@jaihotels.com

recipe page 104

Chateau Elan

100 Rue Charlemagne
Braselton
Georgia 30517
USA

T: +1 678 425 0900
F: +1 770 307 0836
E: reservations
@chateauelan.com

recipe page 100

Careys Manor Hotel

Brockenhurst
New Forest
Hampshire SO42 7RH
England

T: +44 (0)1590 623551
F: +44 (0)1590 622799
E: info@careysmanor.com

recipe page 74

Thurnhers Alpenhof

A-6763 Zürs an Arlberg
Austria

T: +43 5583 2191
F: +43 5583 3330
E: mail@
thurnhers-alpenhof.com

recipe page 64

Down Hall
Country House Hotel

Hatfield Heath
Near Bishops Stortford
Hertfordshire CM22 7AS
England

T: +44 (0)1279 731441
F: +44 (0)1279 730416
E: reception@downhall.co.uk

recipe page 126

Amberley Castle

Amberley
near Arundel
West Sussex BN18 9LT
England

T: +44 (0)1798 831992
F: +44 (0)1798 831998
E: info@amberleycastle.co.uk

recipe page 34

The Elms
Hotel and Restaurant

Stockton Road
Abberley
Worcestershire WR6 6AT
England

T: +44 (0)1299 896666
F: +44 (0)1299 896804
E: info@theelmshotel.co.uk

recipe page 142

Armathwaite Hall Hotel

Bassenthwaite Lake
Keswick
Cumbria CA12 4RE
England

T: +44 (0)1768 776551
F: +44 (0)1768 776220
E: reservations@
armathwaite-hall.com

recipe page 130

Feversham Arms Hotel

Helmsley
North Yorkshire YO62 5AG
England

T: +44 (0)1439 770766
F: +44 (0)1439 770346
E: info@
fevershamarmshotel.com

recipe page 134

Blakes Hotel

33 Roland Gardens
London SW7 3PF
England

T: +44 (0)20 7370 6701
F: +44 (0)20 7373 0442
E: blakes-sales
@blakeshotels.com

recipe page 42

The Gibbon Bridge Hotel

Chipping
Forest of Bowland
Preston, Lancashire PR3 2TQ
England

T: +44 (0)1995 61456
F: +44 (0)1995 61277
E: reception@
gibbon-bridge.co.uk

Green Bough Hotel

60 Hoole Road
Chester
Cheshire CH2 3NL
England
T: +44 (0)1244 326241
F: +44 (0)1244 326265
E: luxury@greenbough.co.uk

recipe page 110

The Priory Bay Hotel

Priory Drive
Seaview
Isle of Wight PO34 5BU
England
T: +44 (0)1983 613146
F: +44 (0)1983 616539
E: enquiries@priorybay.co.uk

recipe page 108

Hazlewood Castle

Paradise Lane
Near Tadcaster
North Yorkshire LS24 9NJ
England
T: +44 (0)1937 535353
F: +44 (0)1937 530630
E: info@
   hazlewood-castle.co.uk

recipe page 138

The Ritz London

150 Piccadilly
London W1J 9BR
England
T: +44 (0)207 493 8181
F: +44 (0)207 493 2687
E: enquire@
   theritzlondon.com

recipe page 40

The Montagu Arms Hotel

Beaulieu
New Forest
Hampshire SO42 7ZL
England
T: +44 (0)1590 612324
F: +44 (0)1590 612188
E: reservations@
   montaguarmshotel.co.uk

recipe page 134

Rosevine Hotel

Portscatho
Roseland, Truro
Cornwall TR2 5EW
England
T: +44 (0)1872 580206
F: +44 (0)1872 580230
E: info@rosevine.co.uk

recipe page 96

**Morston Hall
Hotel and Restaurant**

Morston, Holt
Norfolk NR25 7AA
England
T: +44 (0)1263 741041
F: +44 (0)1263 740419
E: reception@
   morstonhall.com

recipe page 128

Simpson's Restaurant

20 Highfield Road
Edgbaston
Birmingham B15 3DU
England
T: +44 (0)121 454 3434
F: +44 (0)121 454 3399
E: info@
   simpsonsrestaurant.co.uk

recipe page 102

Pendley Manor Hotel

Cow Lane
Tring
Hertfordshire HP23 5QY
England
T: +44 (0)1442 891891
F: +44 (0)1442 890687
E: info@pendley-manor.co.uk

recipe page 46

Soar Mill Cove Hotel

Salcombe
Devon TQ7 3DS
England
T: +44 (0)1548 561566
F: +44 (0)1548 561223
E: info@soarmillcove.co.uk

recipe page 16

Stoke Park Club

Park Road
Stoke Poges
Buckinghamshire SL2 4PG
England
T: +44 (0)1753 717171
F: +44 (0)1753 717181
E: info@stokeparkclub.com

recipe page 132

Winteringham Fields

Winteringham
North Lincolnshire DN15 9PF
England
T: +44 (0)1724 733096
F: +44 (0)1724 733898
E: wintfields@aol.com

recipe page 14

Summer Lodge
Country House Hotel,
Restaurant & Spa

Summer Lane
Evershot, Dorset DT2 0JR
England
T: +44 (0)1935 482000
F: +44 (0)1935 482040
E: summer@
relaischateaux.com

recipe page 52

Domaine Cocagne

Colline de la Route de Vence
30 Chemin du Pain de Sucre
06800 Cagnes-sur-Mer
France
T: +33 4 92 13 57 77
F: +33 4 92 13 57 89
E: hotel@
domainecocagne.com

recipe page 106

Thatched Cottage
Hotel & Restaurant

16 Brookley Road
Brockenhurst
Hampshire SO42 7RR
England
T: +44 (0)1590 623090
F: +44 (0)1590 623479
E: sales@
thatchedcottage.co.uk

recipe page 92

Adare Manor
Hotel & Golf Resort

Adare
County Limerick
Republic of Ireland
T: +353 61 396566
F: +353 61 396124
E: info@adaremanor.com

recipe page 118

The Vineyard
at Stockcross

Stockcross
Newbury
Berkshire RG20 8JU
England
T: +44 (0)1635 528770
F: +44 (0)1635 528398
E: general@
the-vineyard.co.uk

recipe page 88

Ashford Castle

Cong
County Mayo
Republic of Ireland
T: +353 94 9546003
F: +353 94 9546260
E: ashford@ashford.ie

recipe page 54

WILTONS Restaurant

55 Jermyn Street
St James's
London SW1Y 6LX
England
T: +44 (0)207 629 9955
F: +44 (0)207 495 6233
E: wiltons@wiltons.co.uk

recipe page 48

Ballynahinch Castle Hotel

Ballynahinch, Recess
Connemara, County Galway
Republic of Ireland
T: +353 95 31006
F: +353 95 31085
E: bhinch@iol.ie

recipe page 112

Dromoland Castle

Newmarket-on-Fergus
County Clare
Republic of Ireland
T: +353 61 368144
F: +353 61 363355
E: sales@dromoland.ie

recipe page 86

Quinta da Bela Vista

Caminho do Avista Navios, 4
9000-129 Funchal
Madeira
Portugal
T: +351 291 706 410
F: +351 291 706 401
E: info@belavistamadeira.com

recipe page 146

Killashee House Hotel & Villa Spa

Killashee, Naas
County Kildare
Republic of Ireland
T: +353 45 879277
F: +353 45 879266
E: reservations@
   killasheehouse.com

recipe page 18

Hotel Baltschug Kempinski Moscow

Ul. Baltschug 1
115035 Moscow
Russian Federation
T: +7 (501 or 095) 230 6500
F: +7 (501 or 095) 230 6502
E: reservations.baltschug
   @kempinski.com

recipe page 98

Sheen Falls Lodge

Kenmare
County Kerry
Republic of Ireland
T: +353 64 41600
F: +353 64 41386
E: info@sheenfallslodge.ie

recipe page 94

Balinakill Country House

Clachan
Kintyre
Argyll PA29 6XL
Scotland
T: +44 (0)1880 740206
F: +44 (0)1880 740298
E: info@balinakill.com

recipe page 120

Grotta Giusti Natural Spa Resort

Via Grotta Giusti 1411
51015 Monsummano Terme
Pistoia, Tuscany
Italy
T: +39 0572 90771
F: +39 0572 9077200
E: info@grottagiustispa.com

recipe page 60

Cringletie House

Edinburgh Road
Peebles EH45 8PL
Scotland
T: +44 (0)1721 725750
F: +44 (0)1721 725751
E: enquiries@cringletie.com

recipe page 56

Villa Crespi

Via G Fava, 18
28016 Orta San Giulio
Lake d'Orta
Italy
T: +39 322 911 902
F: +39 322 911 919
E: villacrespi@
   lagodortahotels.com

recipe page 22

Norton House

Ingliston
Edinburgh EH28 8LX
Scotland
T: +44 (0)131 333 1275
F: +44 (0)131 333 3752
E: nortonhouse@
   handpicked.co.uk

recipe page 82

recipe page 36

**The Roman Camp Country
House and Restaurant**

Callander
Perthshire FK17 8BG
Scotland
T: +44 (0)1877 330003
F: +44 (0)1877 331533
E: mail@
    roman-camp-hotel.co.uk

recipe page 72

**St Andrews Bay
Golf Resort & Spa**

St Andrews
Fife KY16 8PN
Scotland
T: +44 (0)1334 837000
F: +44 (0)1334 471115
E: info@standrewsbay.com

recipe page 44

**Gran Meliá Salinas
- The Garden Villas**

Avda. Islas Canarias s/n
35509 Costa Teguise
Lanzarote, Canary Islands
Spain
T: +34 928 590040
F: +34 928 591110
E: gran.melia.salinas
    @solmelia.com

recipe page 12

Hotel d'Angleterre

Quai du Mont-Blanc 17
1201 Geneva
Switzerland
T: +41 22 906 5555
F: +41 22 906 5556
E: angleterre@rchmail.com

INDEX OF RECIPES

Crispy fried dragon prawns with mandarin orange coriander salsa,
longan filled with prawn and chilli salsa on lime jelly 26

duck: New Forest duckling with aubergine and honey sauce. 92

    roast breast of duck, green beans and fresh almonds,
      seared foie gras, argan oil and white peach 94

eel: salad of smoked and smoked trout sausage on a potato pancake 70

Egg noodle wrapped tiger prawns with exotic fruit tian 24

eggs: trio of scrambled with vegetable crisp and Parmesan fingers 12

Fillet of Kintyre sika venison with Parisienne potatoes and a red wine reduction 120

Fillet of Lamb with char-grilled Provençal vegetables, garlic rösti and a rosemary jus 108

Fillet of red mullet on a pea risotto with lemon and thyme Mascarpone 64

Fillet of wild salmon freshly smoked on turf with a cream sauce of fresh tarragon 54

foie gras: and panaché of roasted scallops, sauce Sauternes 36

      mosaic, apple jelly, fig and prune chutney 82

Gingerbread and chocolate pudding,
St Lucian vanilla ice cream and sun blushed pineapples and chilli 144

Grenadin of local veal with wild mushroom and Madeira jus,
celeriac and potato dauphinoise and baby vegetables 96

Grilled pepper tuna with Portobello and tomato ragout,
organic fresh greens, coriander jus 62

halibut: roast fillet, saffron potatoes, smoked haddock chowder foam 46

Individual cheesecakes with raspberry coulis 140

John Dory 'Demi-Deuil' with a cappuccino of truffle butter and chablis   68

lamb: cannon of salt marsh Welsh, fondant potato,
     leek and courgette spaghetti, shiraz, mint and rosemary reduction   110

     fillet with char-grilled Provençal vegetables, garlic rösti and a rosemary jus   108

     pecan crusted ribeye, wild mountain greens, sweet potato charlotte,
     port wine and fig demi glace   104

     stuffed saddle   106

liquorice: yummy pannacotta with frozen berries and a sabayon swirl   138

Lobster escabèche with candied olives and black olive emulsion   38

lobster: butter poached with cardamom, coriander and basmati rice   40

     Caribbean and plantain wrapped Anegada Mahi Mahi,
     mango gastrique, coriander oil   76

mahi mahi: plantain wrapped Anegada,
     Caribbean lobster and mango gastrique, coriander oil   76

Medallions of rabbit saddle and black pudding wrapped in bacon,
wholegrain mustard sauce   118

Mosaic of foie gras, apple jelly, fig and prune chutney   82

mullet: fillet of red on a pea risotto with lemon and thyme Mascarpone   64

     pan fried red tart with salad of tomato and aubergine caviar,
     baby mozzarella with pesto and balsamico dressing   66

Mussel soup with saffron sprigs   20

New Forest duckling with aubergine and honey sauce.   92

Ostrich fillet parcels   116

Pan fried red mullet tart with salad of tomato and aubergine caviar,
baby mozzarella with pesto and balsamico dressing   66

Panaché of roasted scallops and foie gras, sauce Sauternes   36

Pandan pudding with blueberry compote 136

Peach Melba on almond biscuit 128

Pecan crusted lamb ribeye, wild mountain greens,
sweet potato charlotte, port wine and fig demi glace 104

Plantain wrapped Anegada Mahi Mahi,
Caribbean lobster and mango gastrique, coriander oil 76

pork belly: slow braised wrapped in Parma ham, fricassée of white beans,
squid, garlic, parsley, lemon confit, creamed lobster sauce 102

slow cooked, whole grain mustard crust, potato purée and broad beans 100

Poussin breast and confit leg with shallot tart and foie gras velouté 88

prawns: crispy fried dragon with mandarin orange coriander salsa,
longan filled with prawn and chilli salsa on lime jelly 26

tiger and seared crayfish with spiced coconut curry cream 30

tiger, egg noodle wrapped with exotic fruit tian 24

quail: roasted with tortellini of wild mushrooms, porcini and truffle sauce 114

terrine with herb and black pepper jelly, carrot and poppyseed dressing 112

rabbit: medallions of saddle and black pudding wrapped in bacon,
wholegrain mustard sauce 118

Rainbow maki and tempura bento box 78

Ravioli with raw scampi, tomato filtering and Caciottina cheese 22

Rhubarb meringue tart 134

Roast breast of duck, green beans and fresh almonds,
seared foie gras, argan oil and white peach 94

Roast fillet of halibut, saffron potatoes, smoked haddock chowder foam 46

Roast poussin, étuvée of pak choi and puy lentils, truffle sauce 86

Roasted quail with tortellini of wild mushrooms, porcini and truffle sauce 114

Roasted wild Scottish salmon with a shellfish, chorizo and white bean cassoulet 56

Rosette of tiger shrimp with sesame butter 32

Terrine of quail with herb and black pepper jelly, carrot and poppyseed dressing	112
Trio of marinated Scottish salmon with cucumber, crème fraîche and caviar	52
Trio of scrambled eggs with vegetable crisp and Parmesan fingers	12
Triple dish of veal with Périgord truffles and American artichoke stew	98
Tropical Lady poulet	90
trout: salad of smoked sausage and smoked eel on a potato pancake	70
tuna: baked with Mediterranean herbs and a fish gravy with saffron pistils	60
grilled pepper with Portobello and tomato ragout, organic fresh greens, coriander jus	62
yellowfin ceviche with homegrown coconut water, West Indian Scotch Bonnet chillies and organic herbs	58
Turbot squares on a seafood and asparagus bed	44
veal: grenadin with wild mushroom and Madeira jus, celeriac and potato dauphinoise and baby vegetables	96
triple dish with Périgord truffles and American artichoke stew	98
venison: fillet with Parisienne potatoes and a red wine reduction	120
springbok fillet carpaccio	122
White chocolate truffle with raspberries encased in a thin chocolate shell topped with blood orange ripple ice cream	142
Wild sea bass, colcannon, Pommery mustard ice-cream and red wine reduction	72
Yellowfin tuna ceviche with homegrown coconut water, West Indian Scotch Bonnet chillies and organic herbs	58
Yummy liquorice pannacotta with frozen berries and a sabayon swirl	138

www.chefsofdistinction.com